Halloween Roots

Part 3

A coloring adventure for all

Jeanette Wummel

Coloring Tip:

When coloring with markers place a piece of paper between pages to prevent bleeding to your next design.

Acknowledgments

Thank you for all your support! Because of people like you, you make me want to continue to create art with the world. You are awesome!

Follow me

Facebook:
www.facebook.com/TheRootsofDesign

Facebook Group:
www.facebook.com/group/ColoringRoots

Instagram:
www.instagram.com/therootsofdesign

Twitter:
https://twitter.com/Roots_Of_Design

Etsy:
www.RootsDesign.Etsy.com

Website/Blog:
www.TheRootsofDesign.com

Copyright

Published and Manufactured in the United States
www.TheRootsOfDesign.com

Designs: Jeanette Wummel

ISBN-13: 978-0-9982152-8-0

This Book Belongs To:

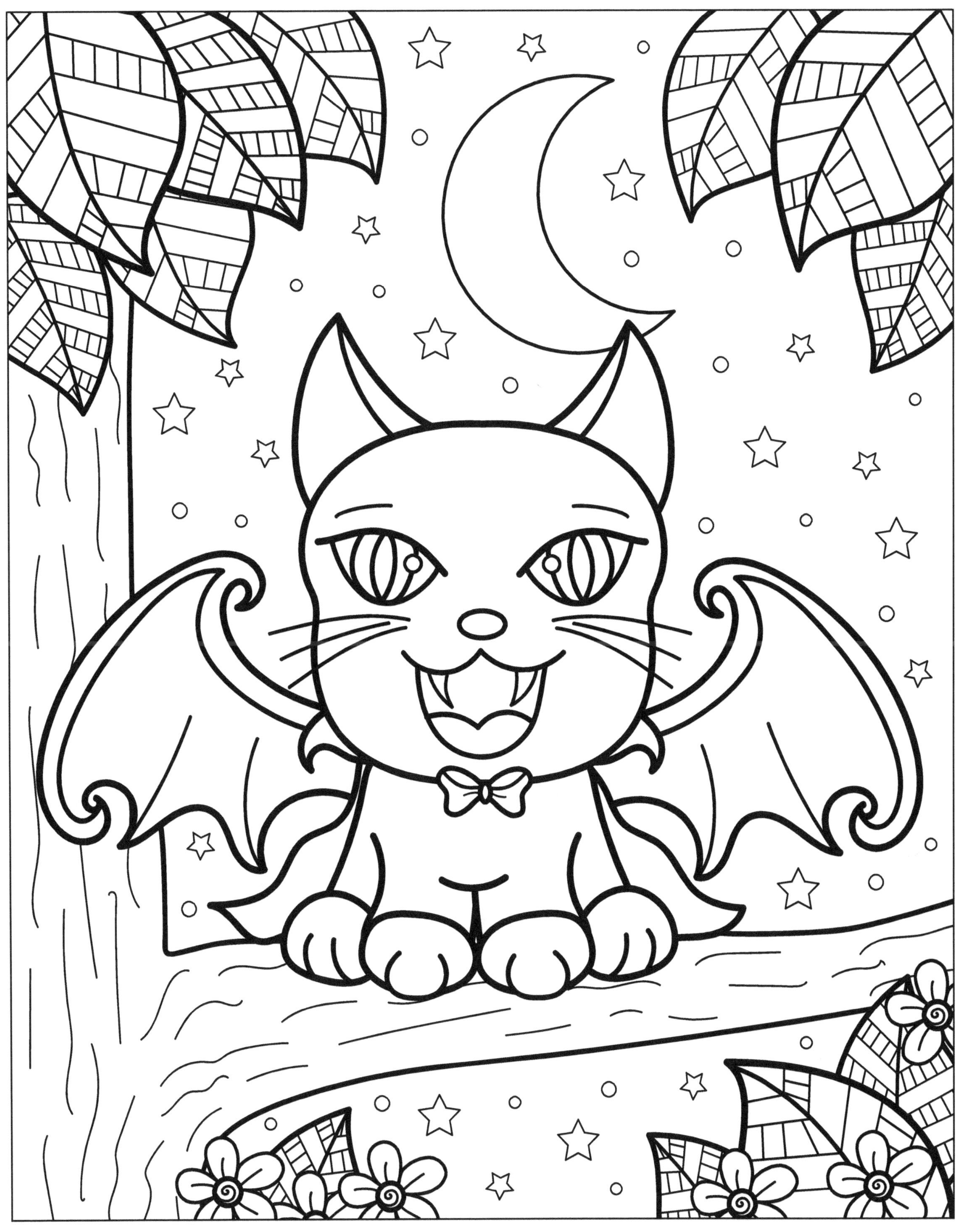

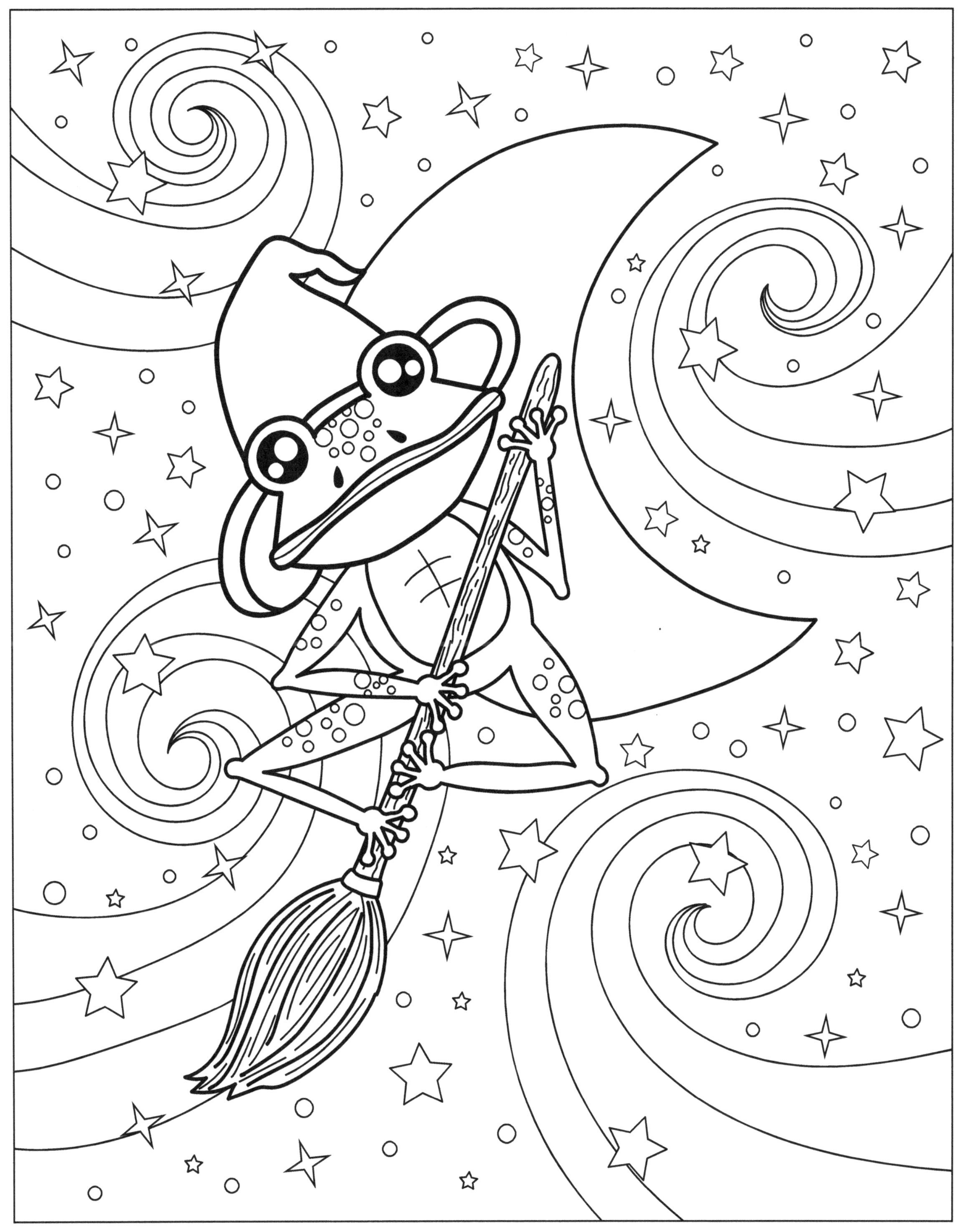

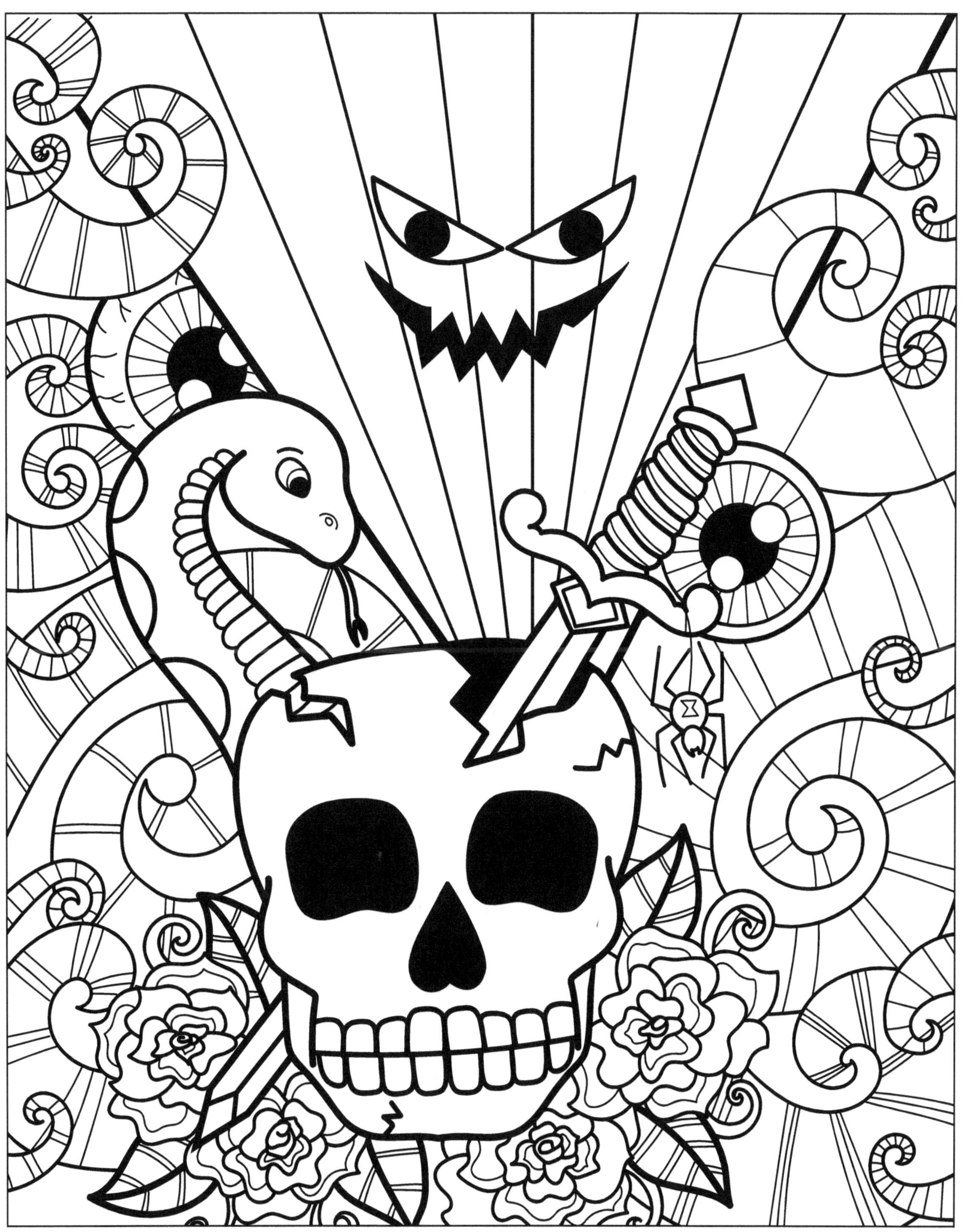

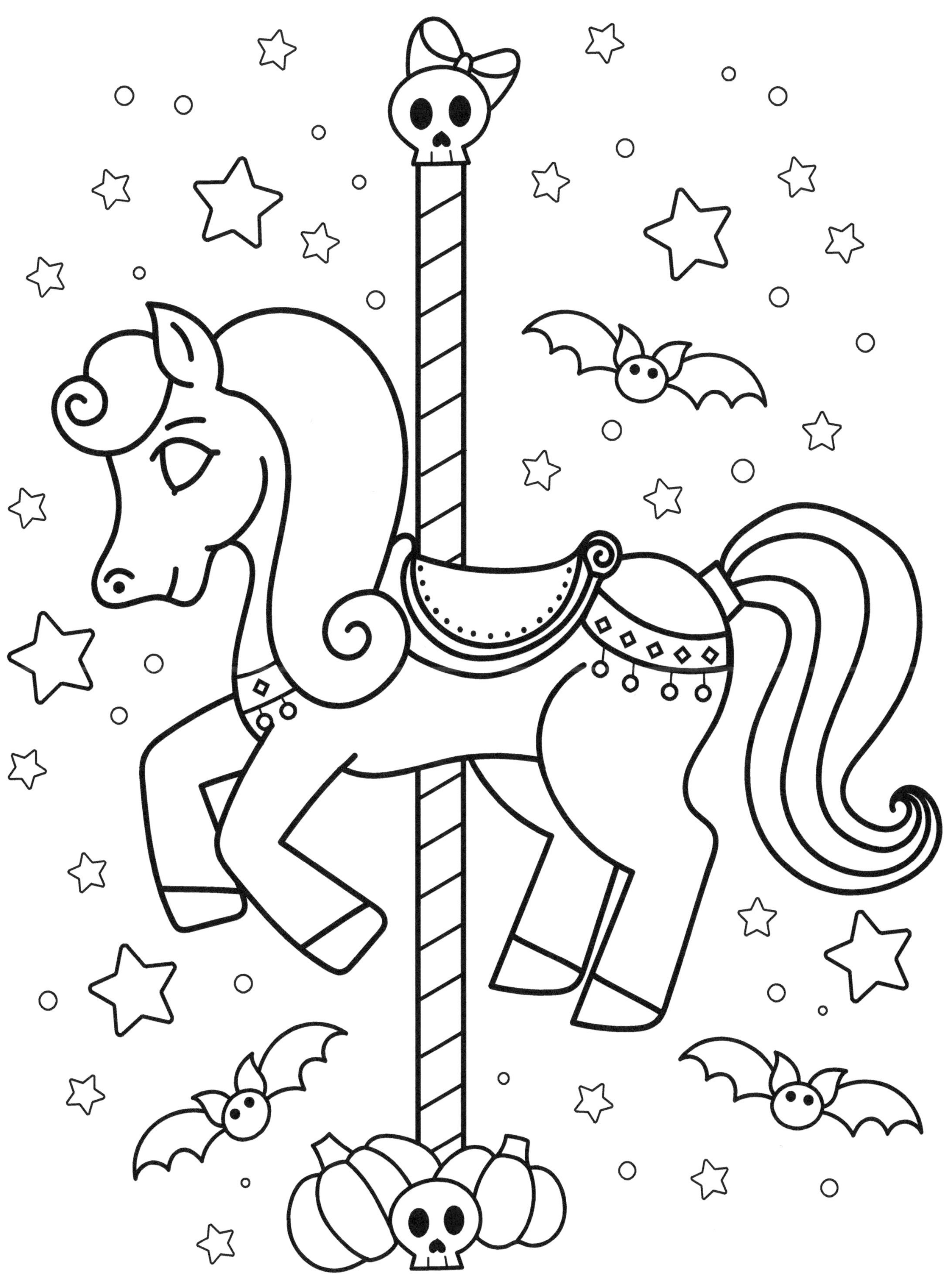

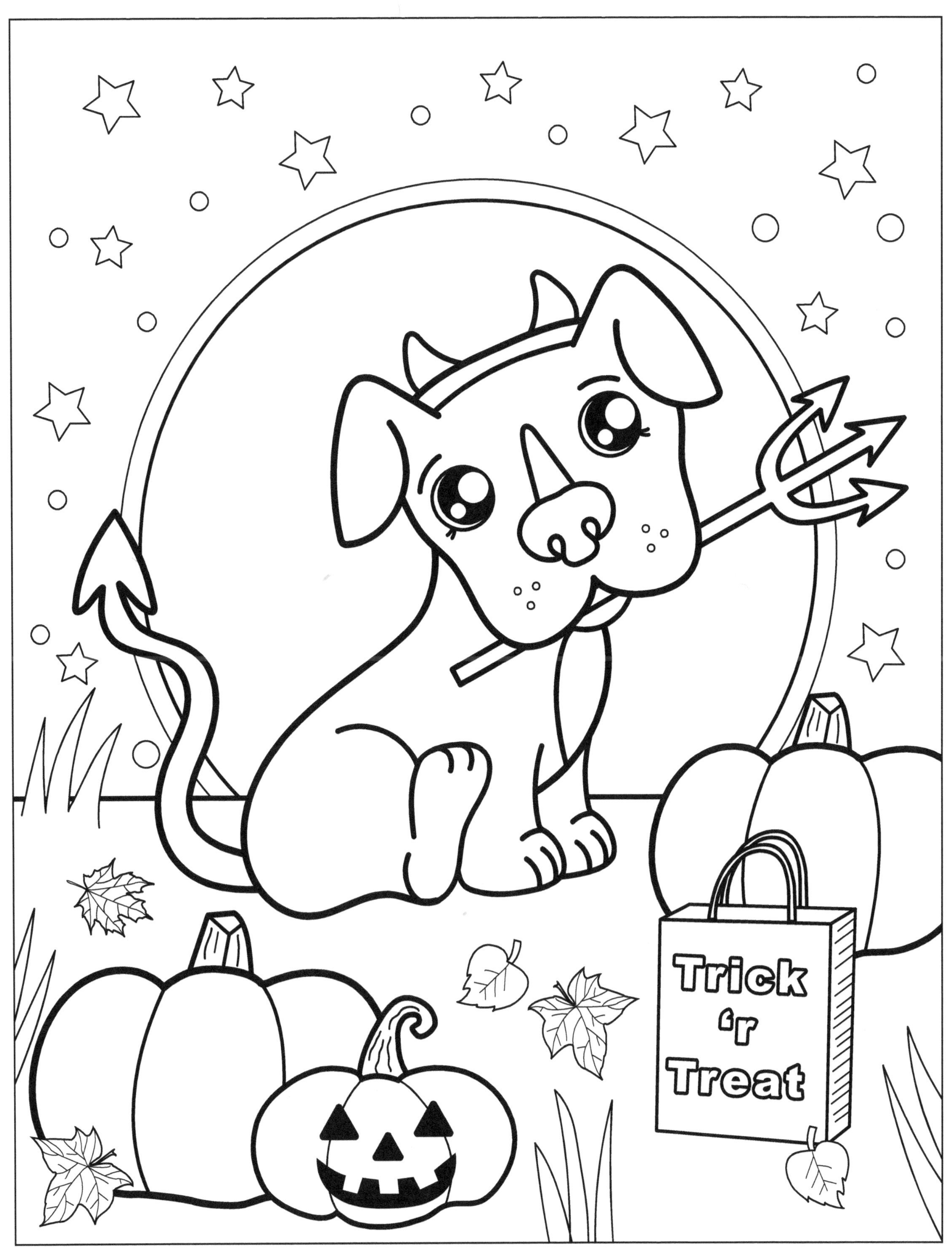
Trick
'r
Treat

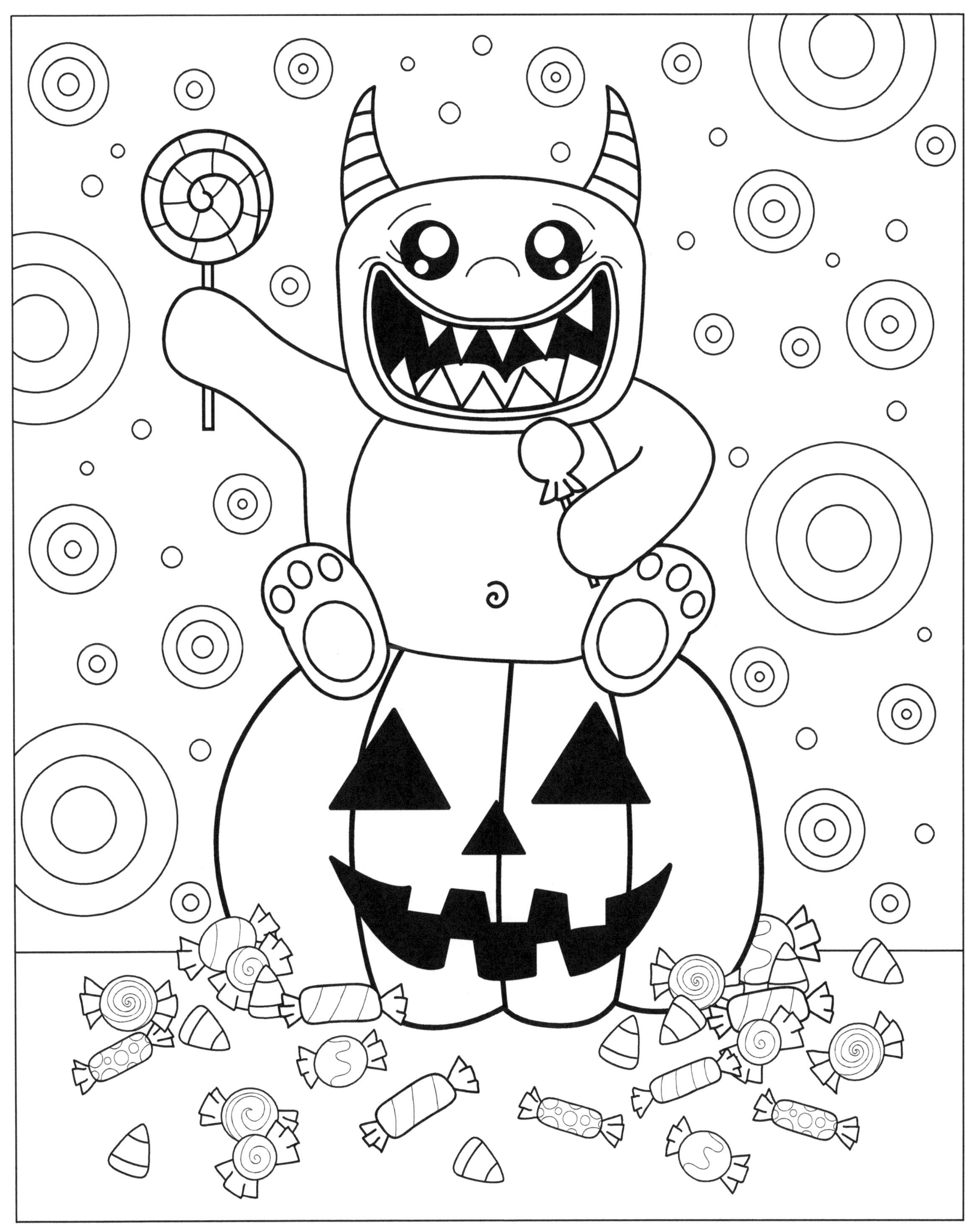

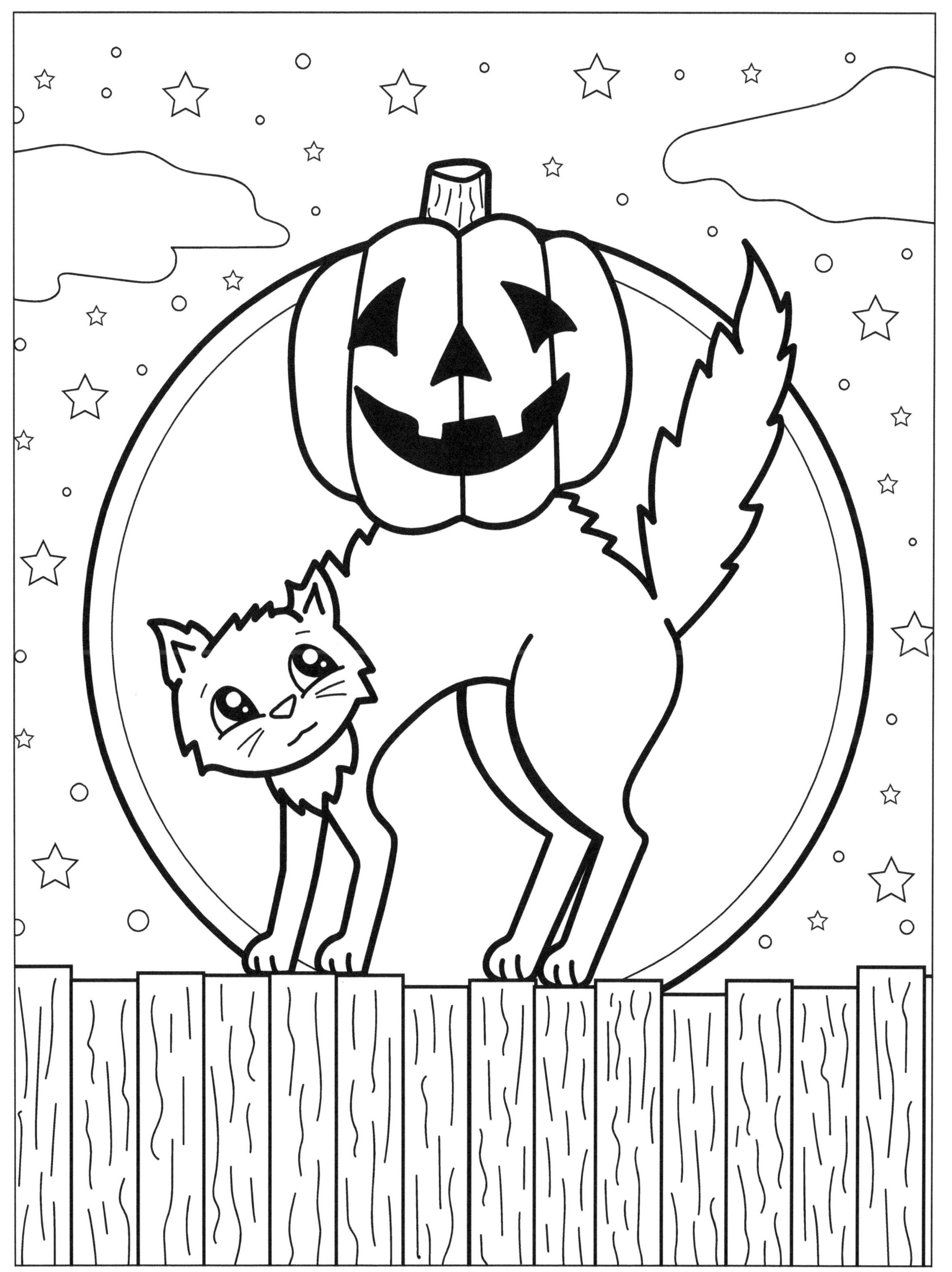

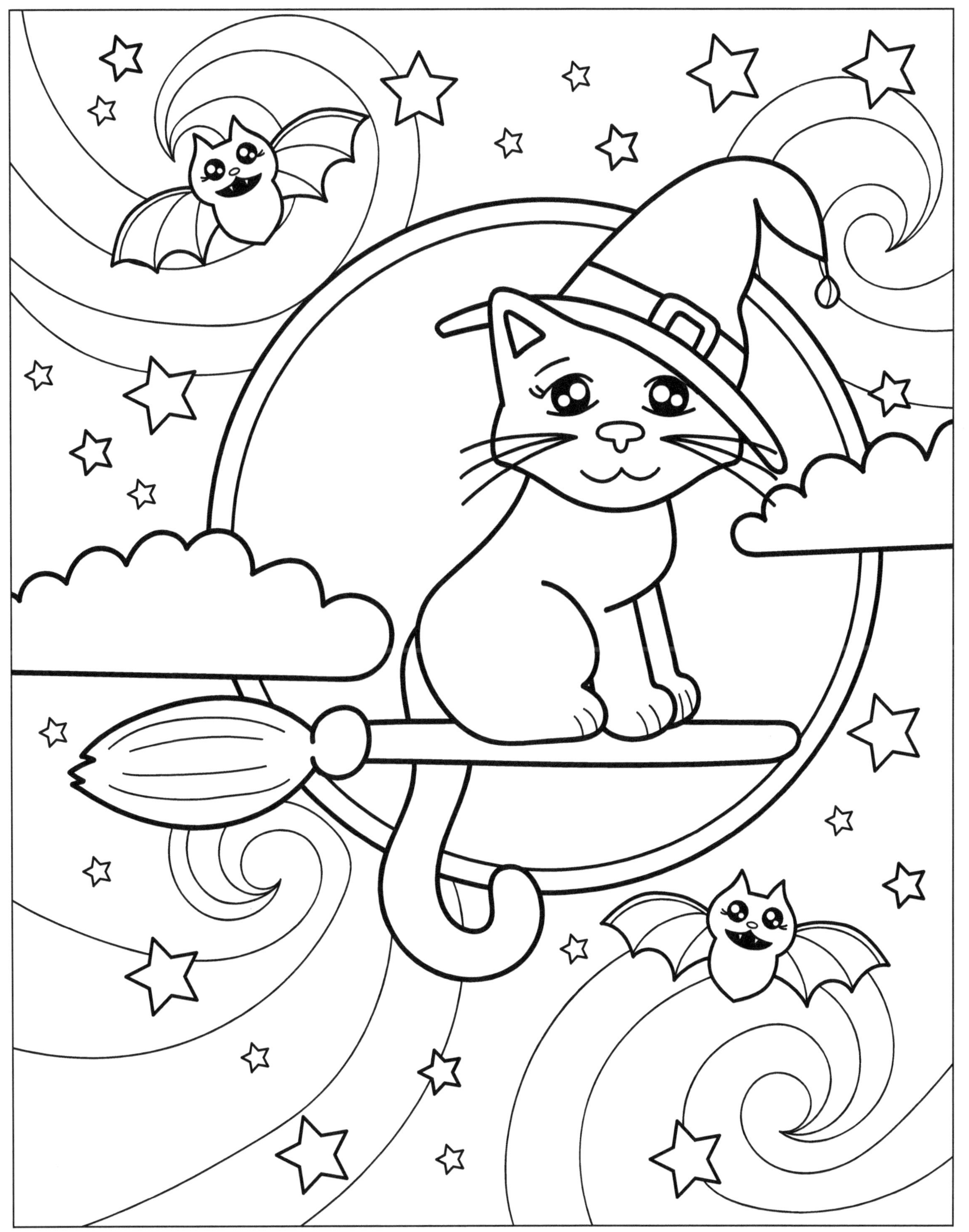

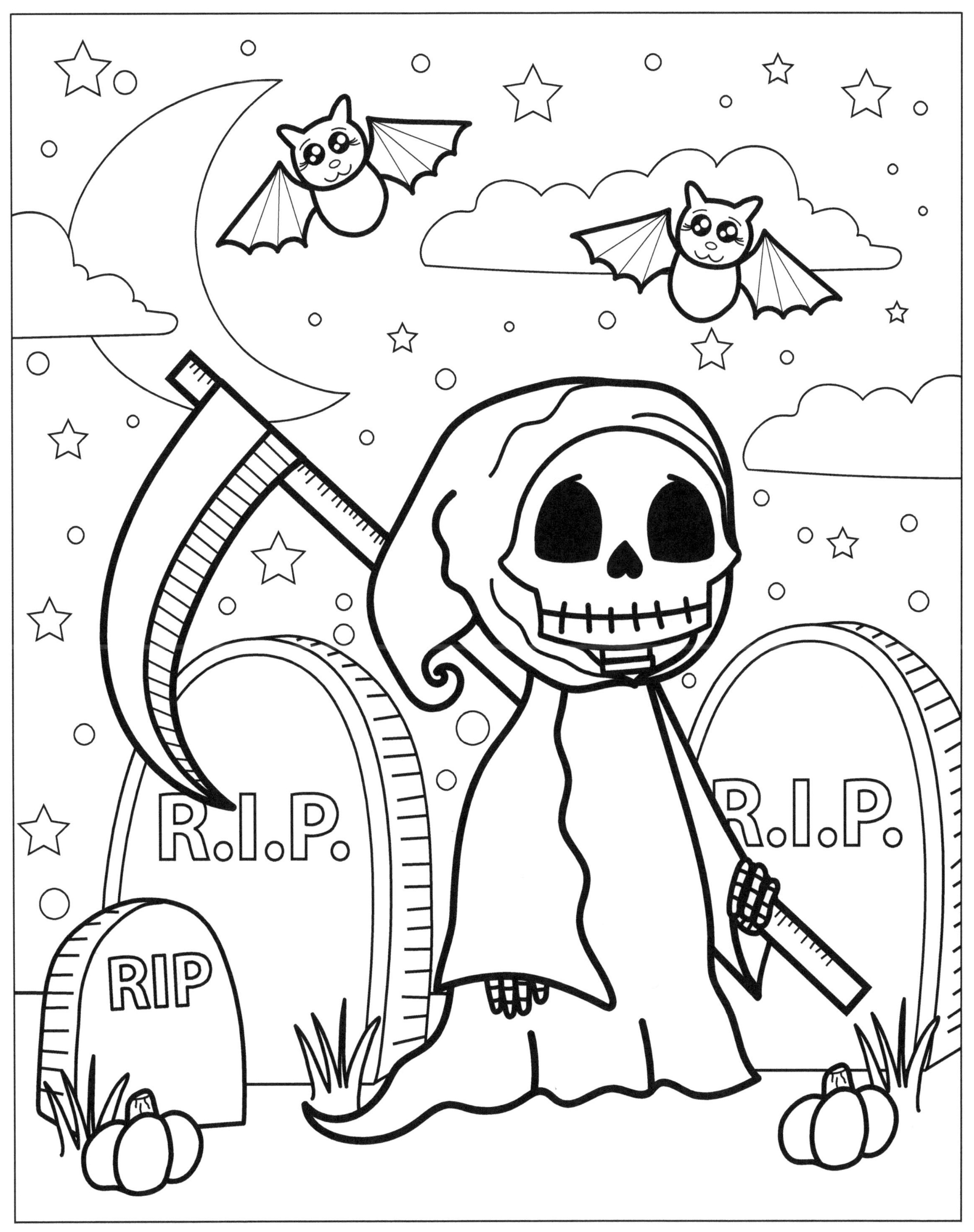
R.I.P.
R.I.P.
RIP

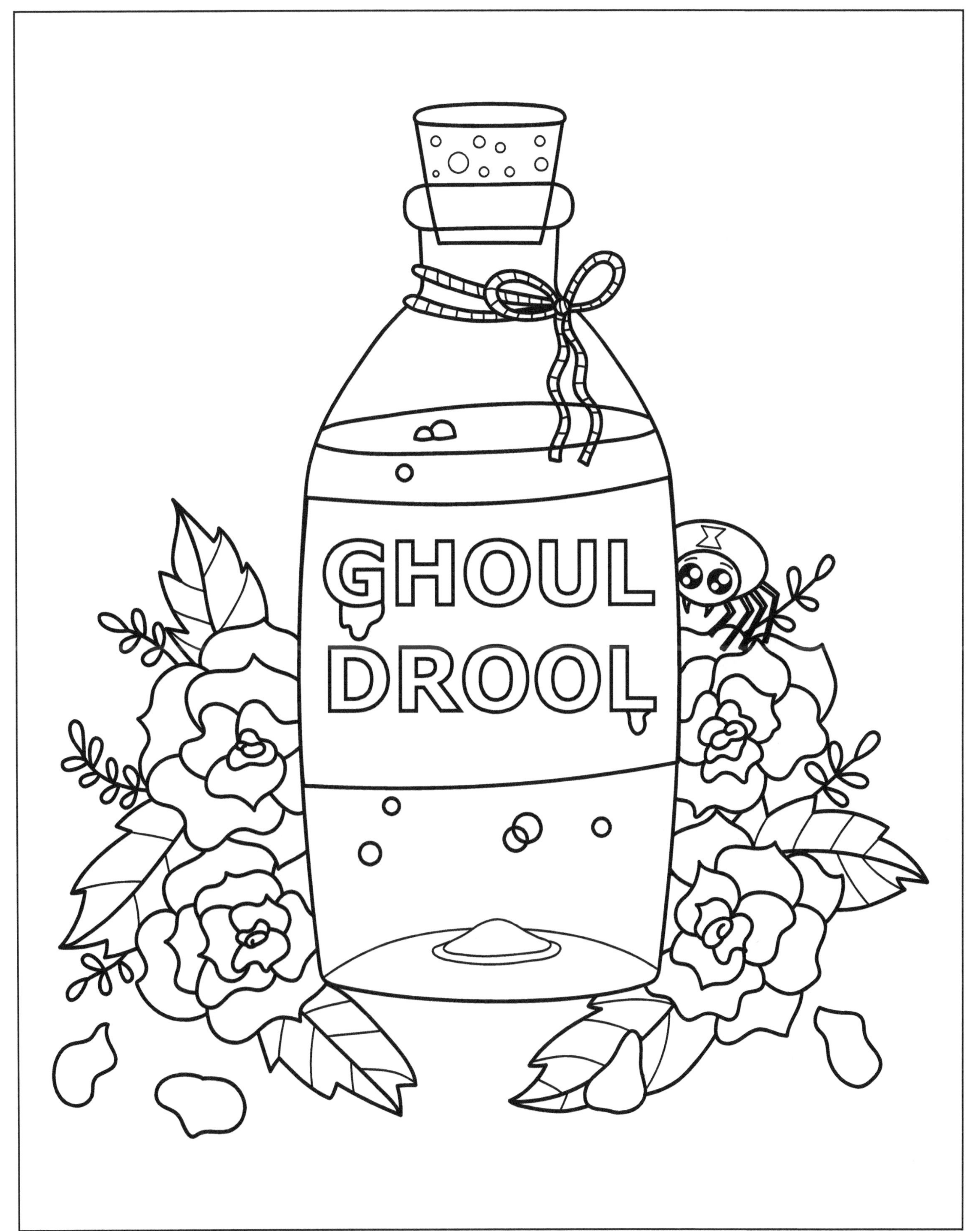
GHOUL
DROOL

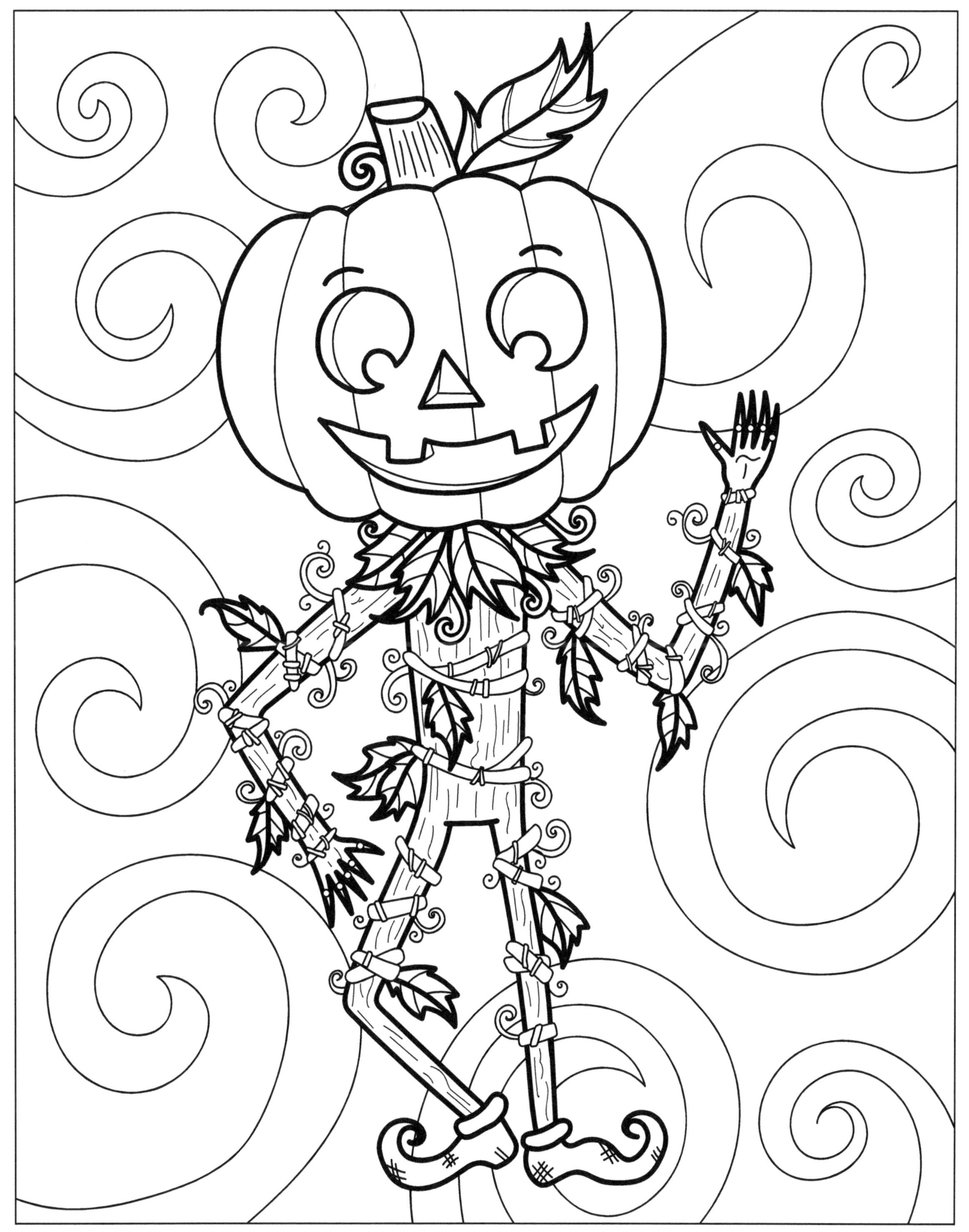

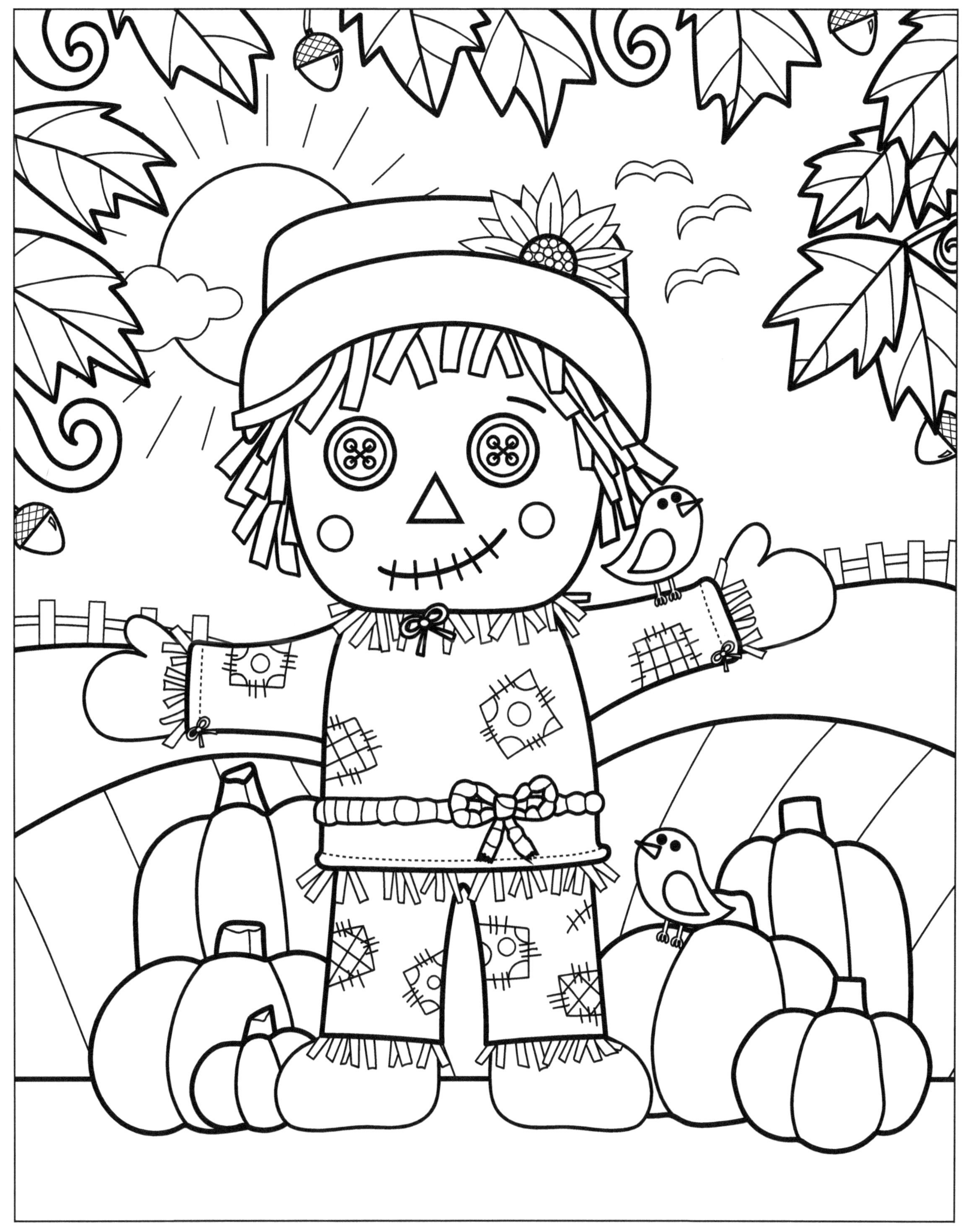

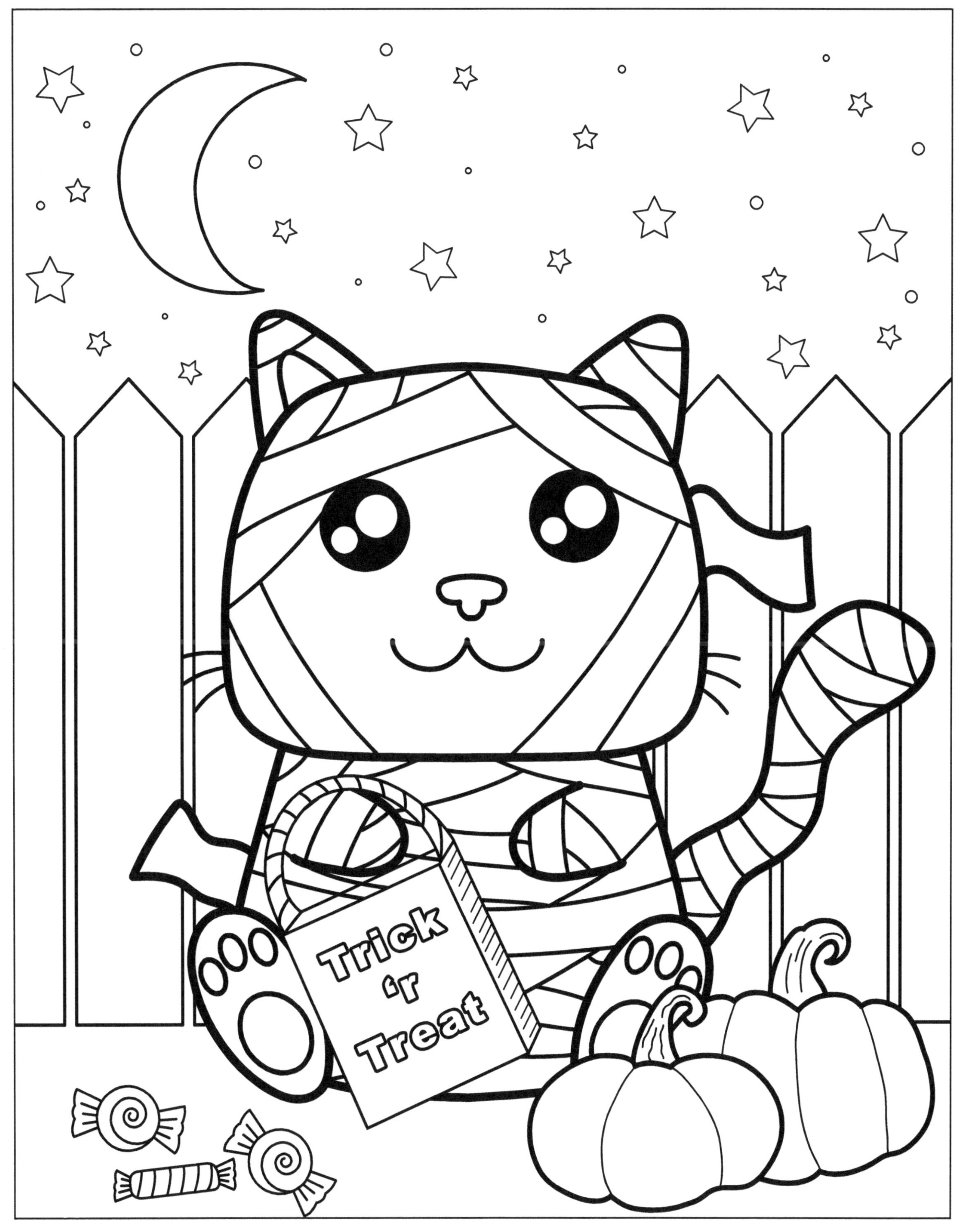
Trick
'r
Treat

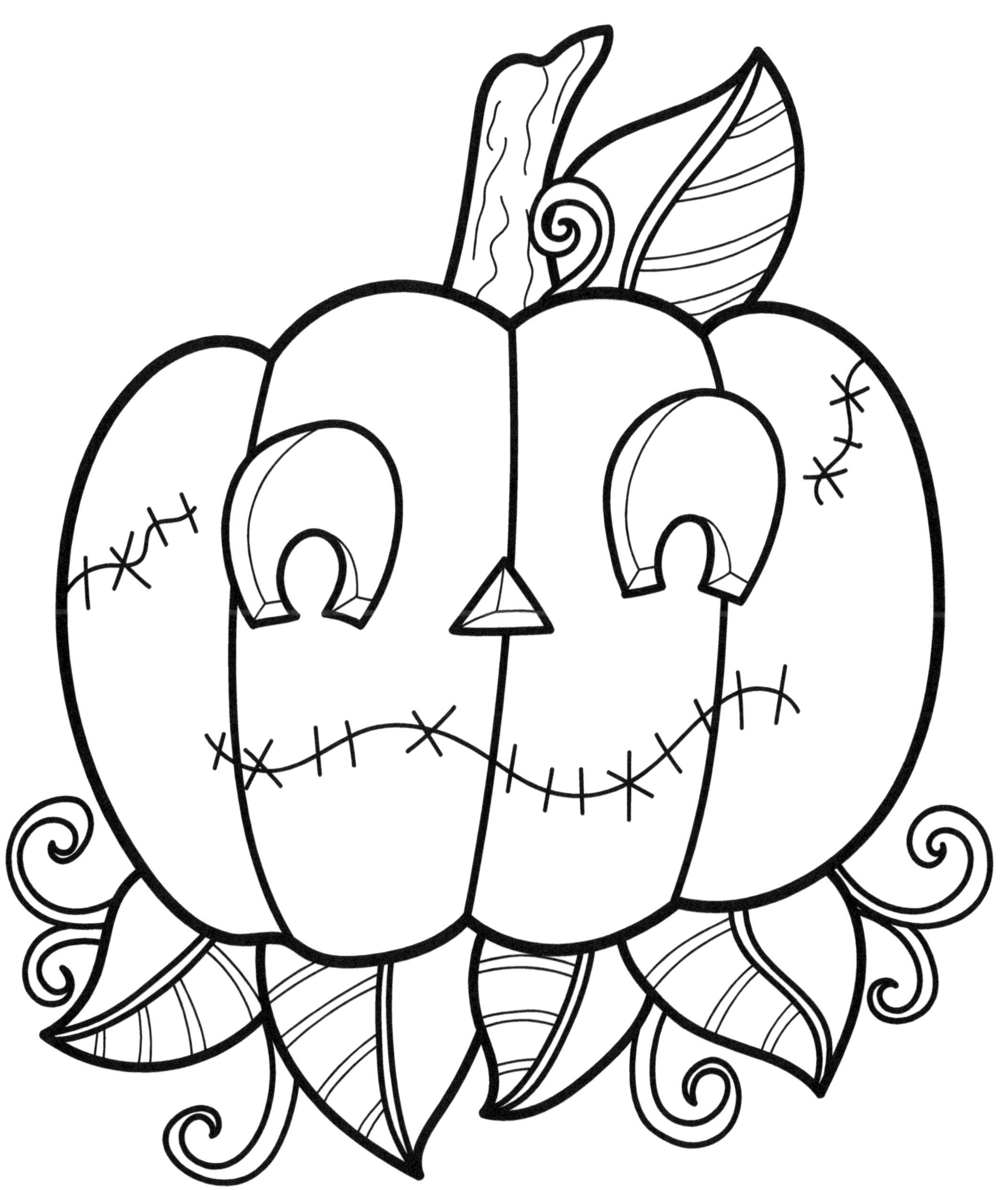

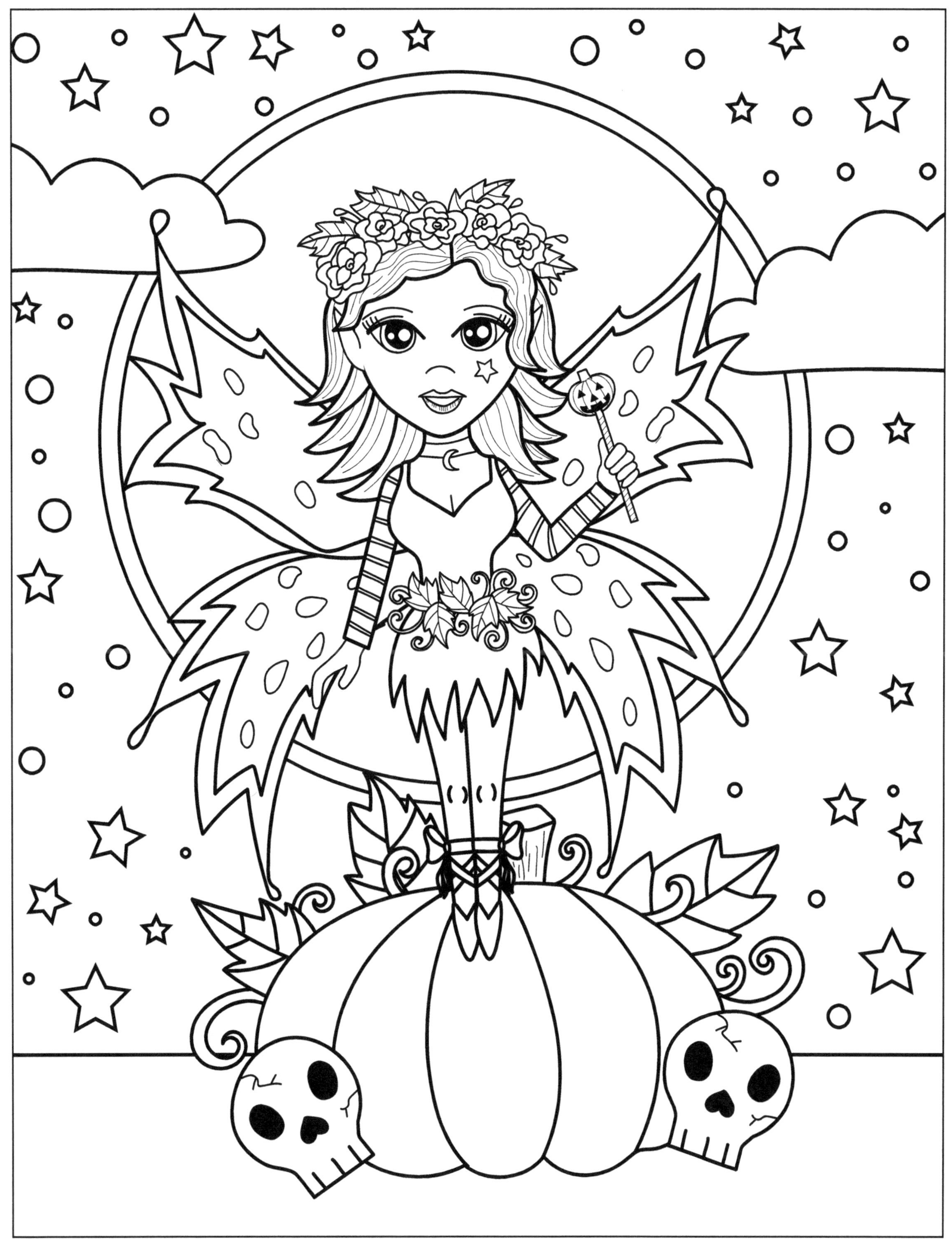

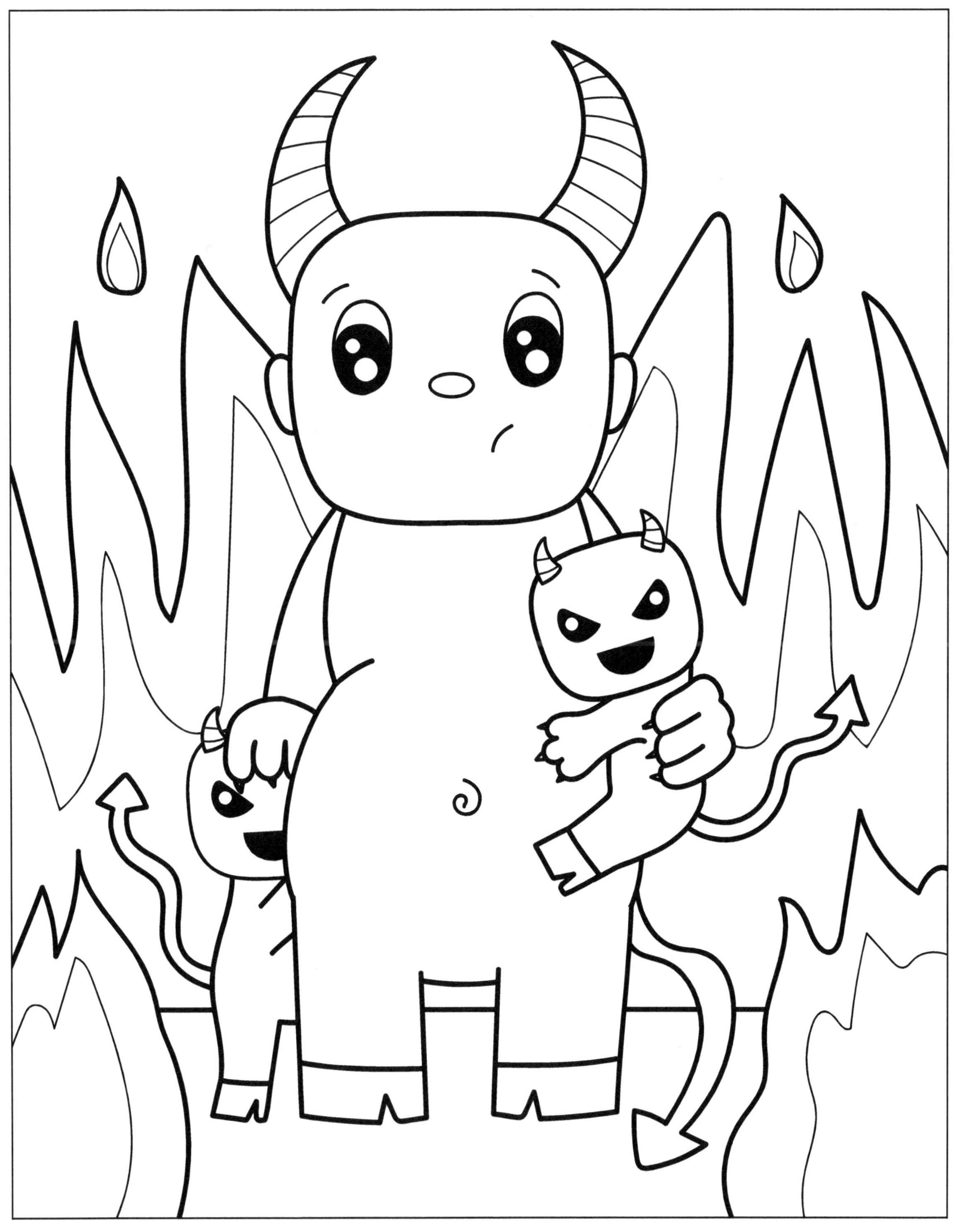

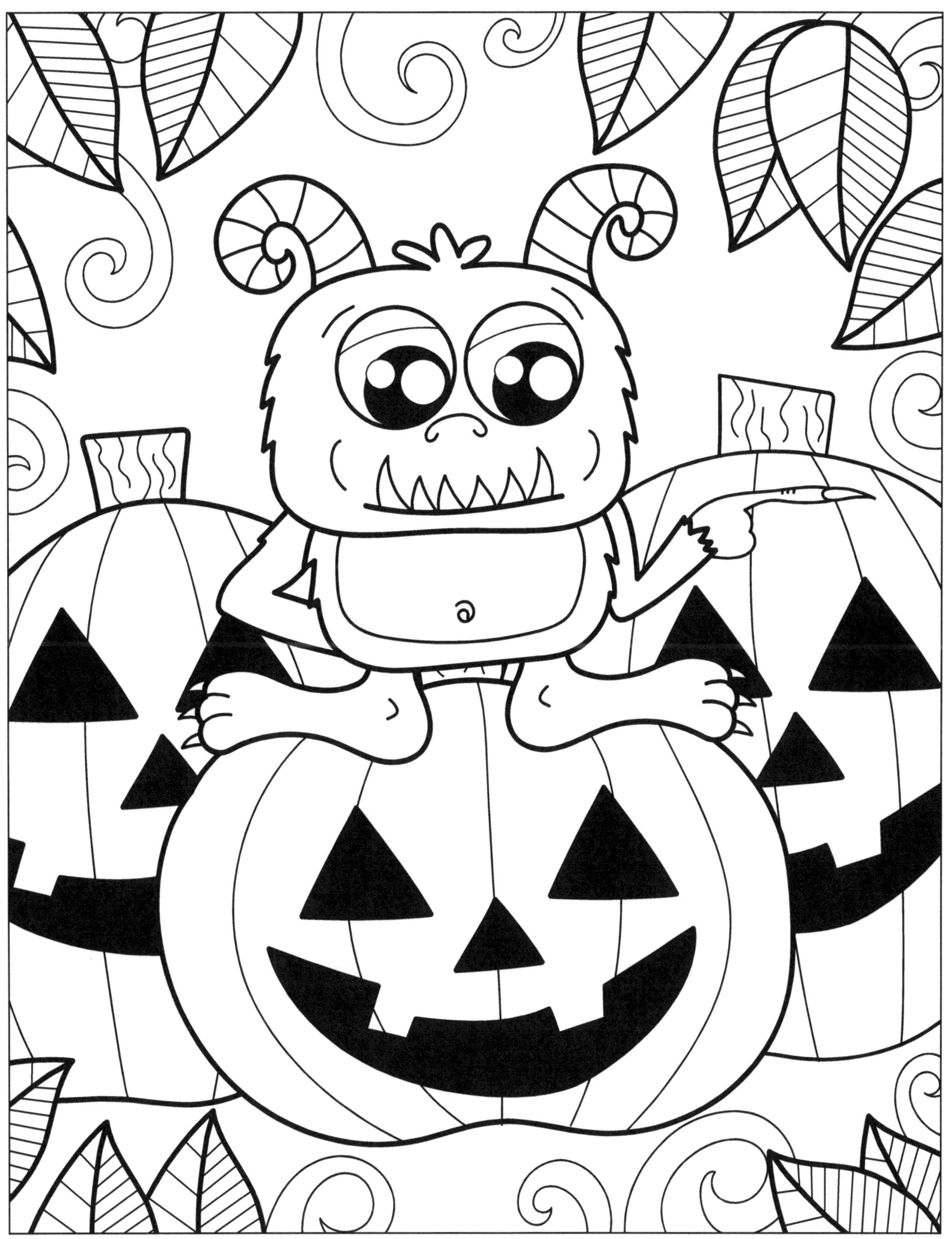

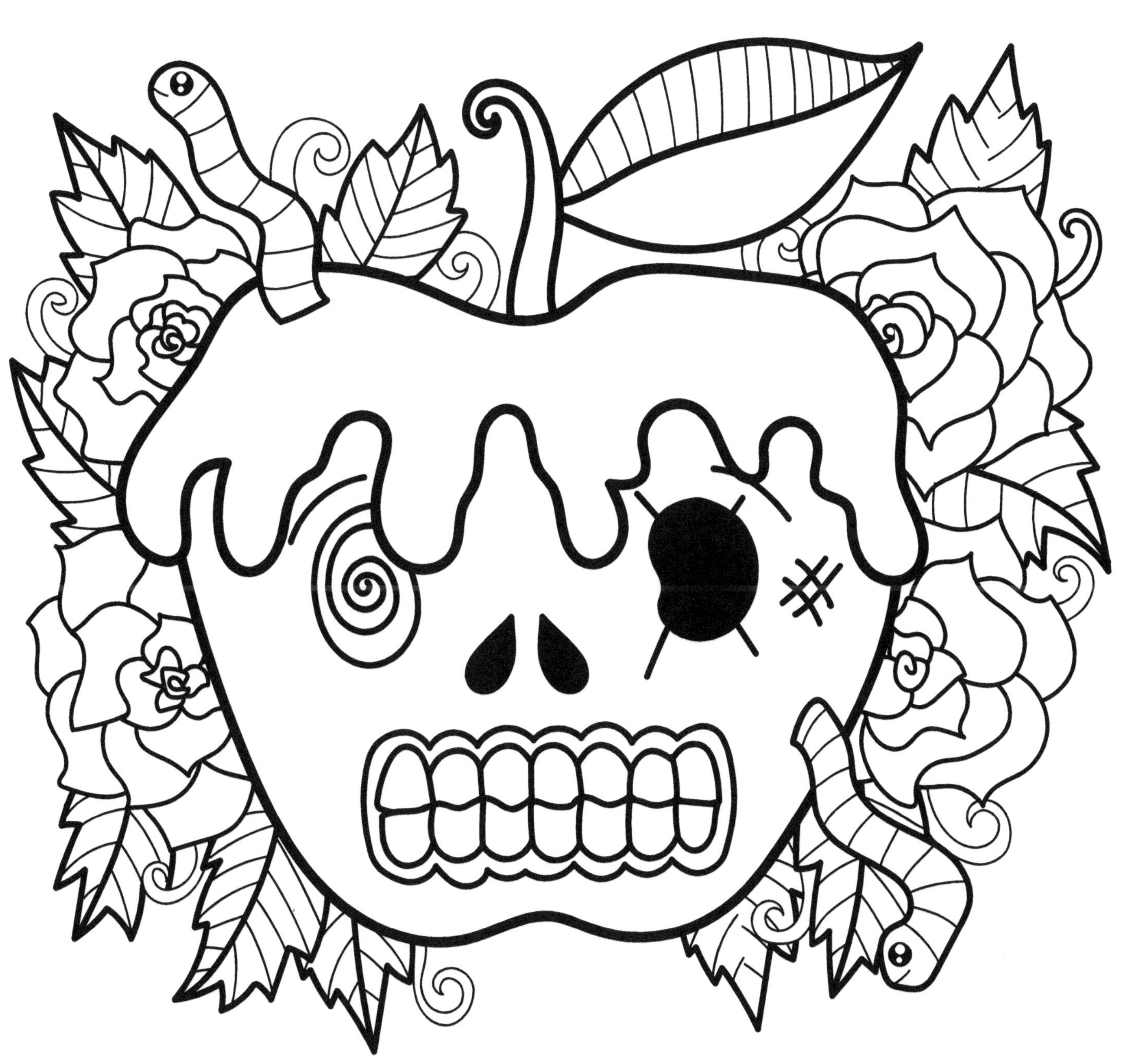

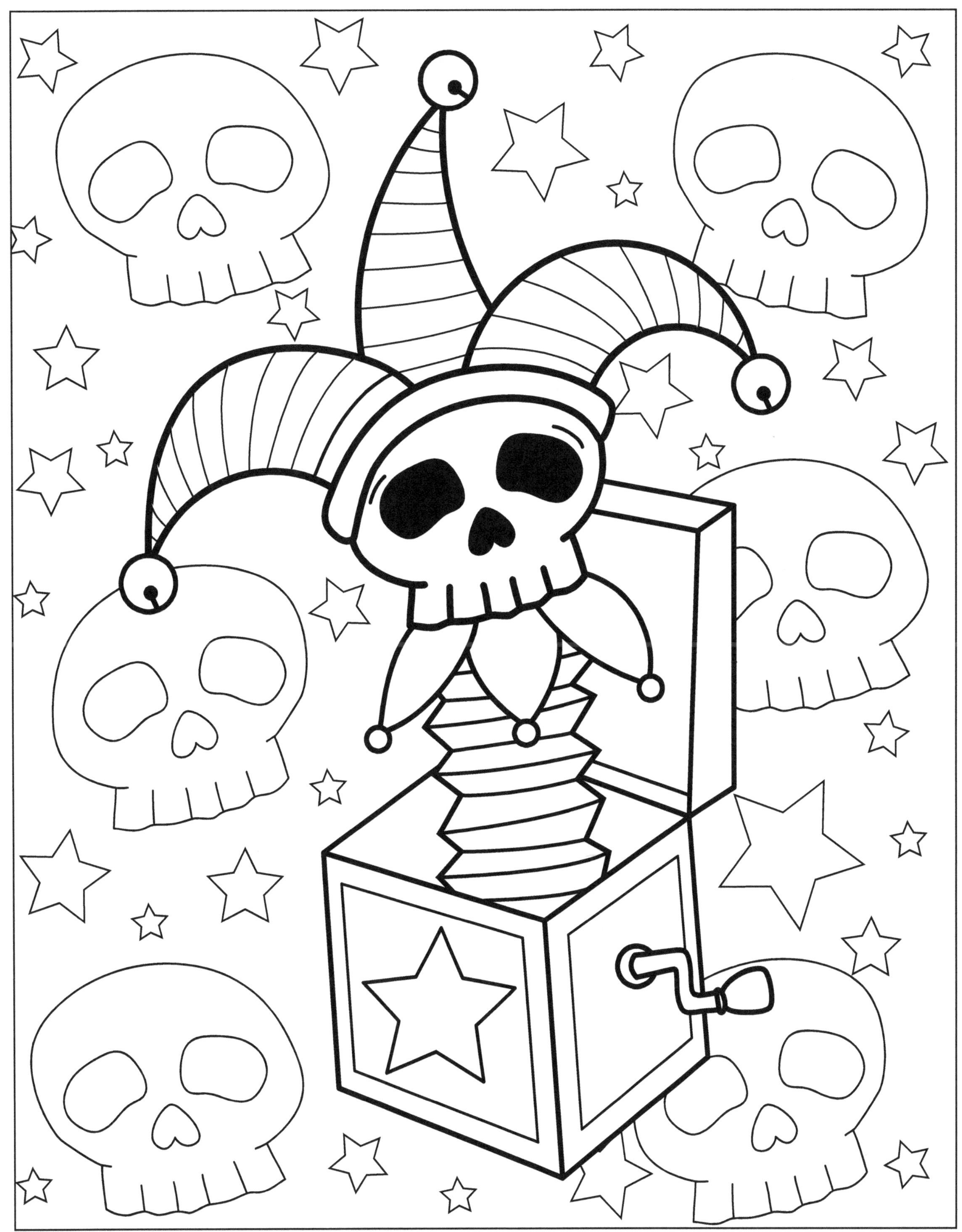

Bonus Pages

The following pages are some of the previous designs, but done in midnight style printed on black pages for your enjoyment.

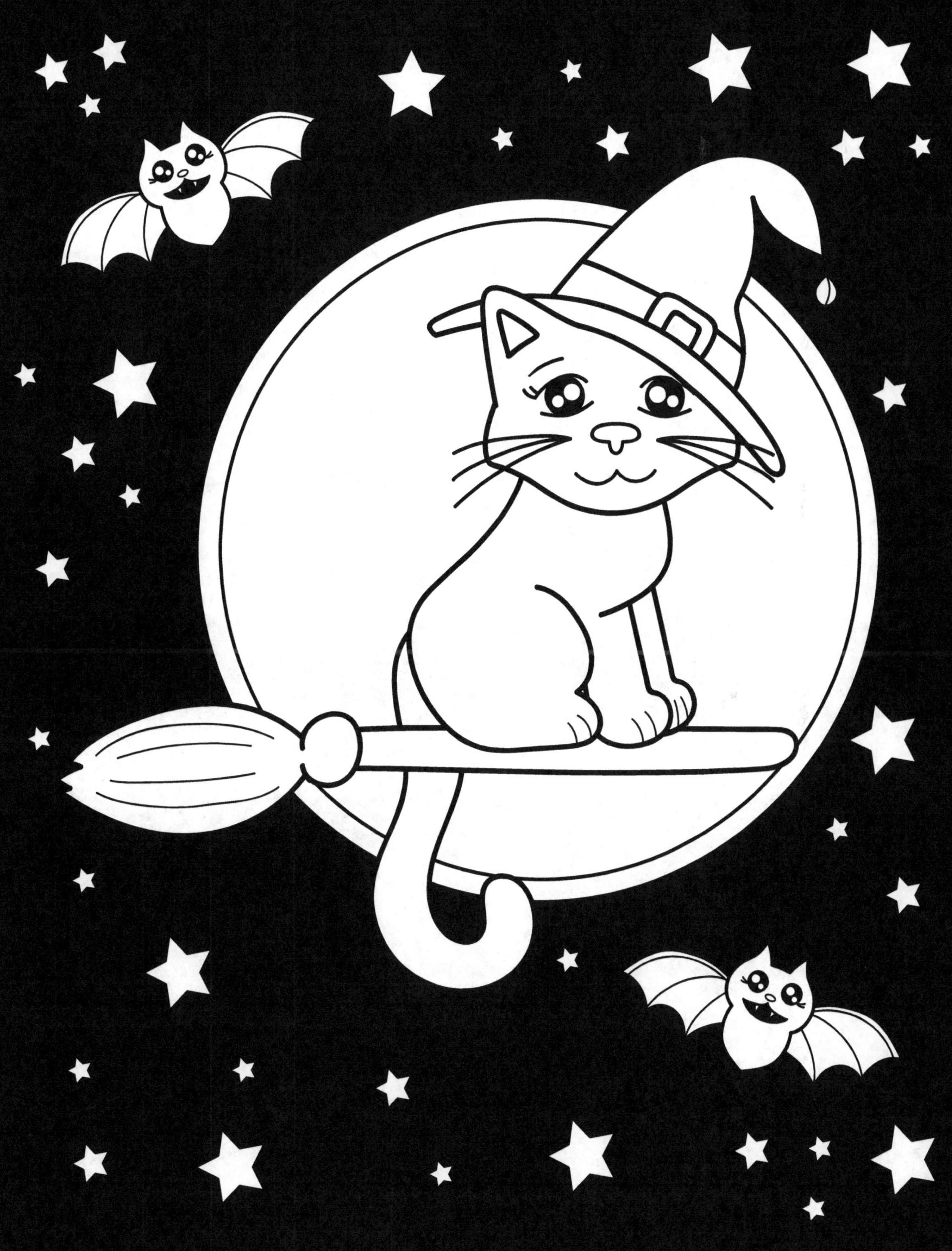

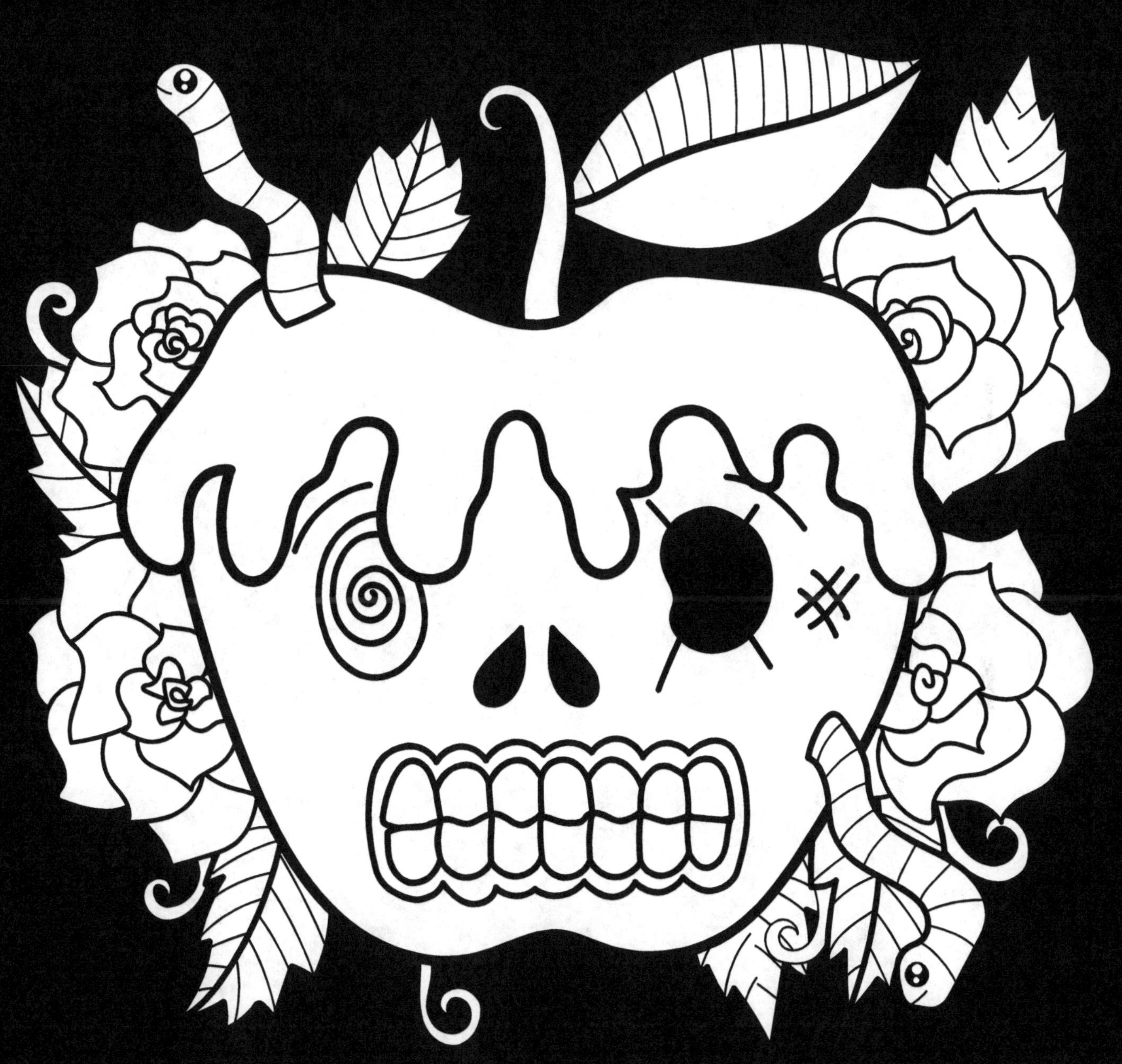

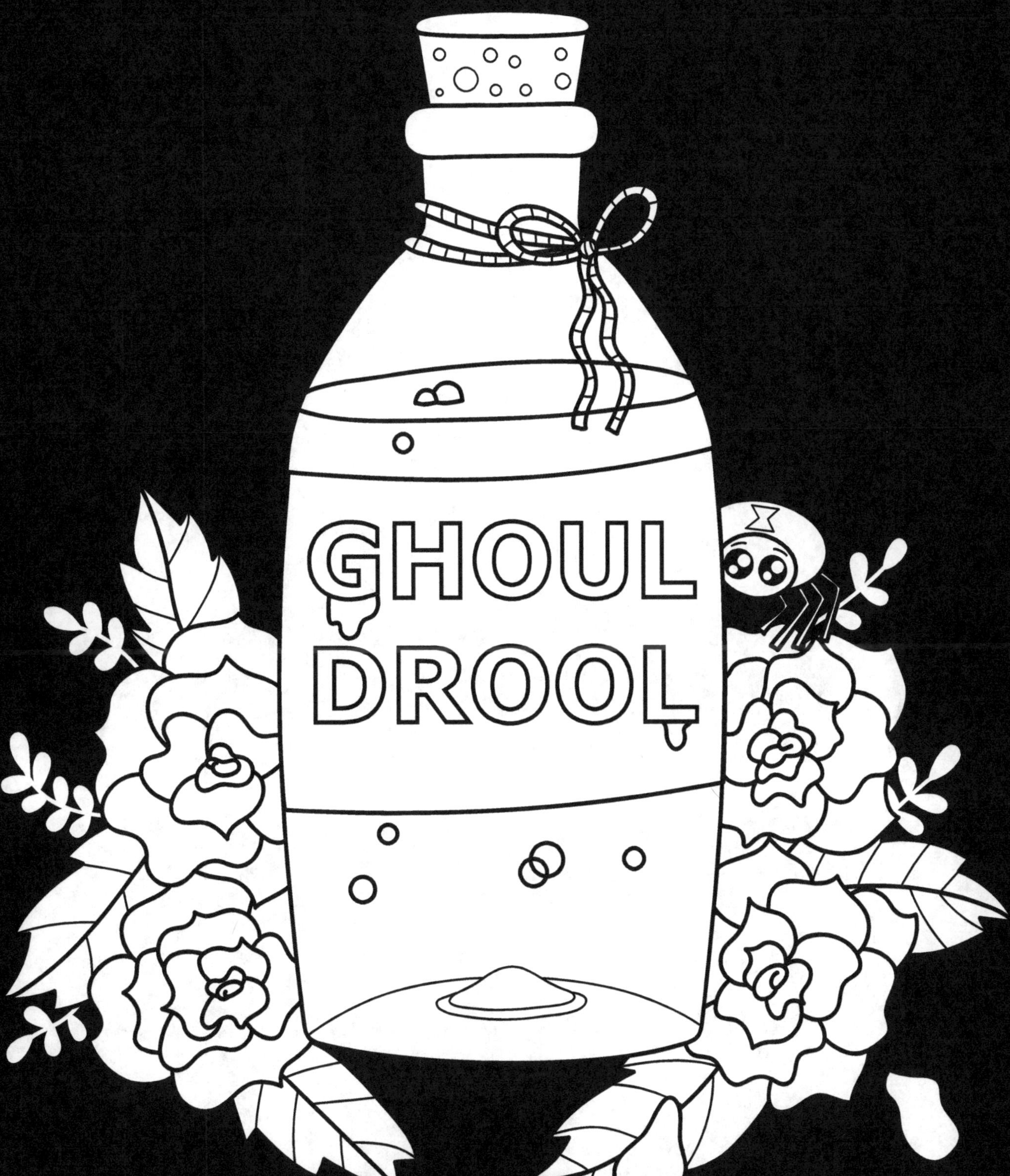
GHOUL
DROOL

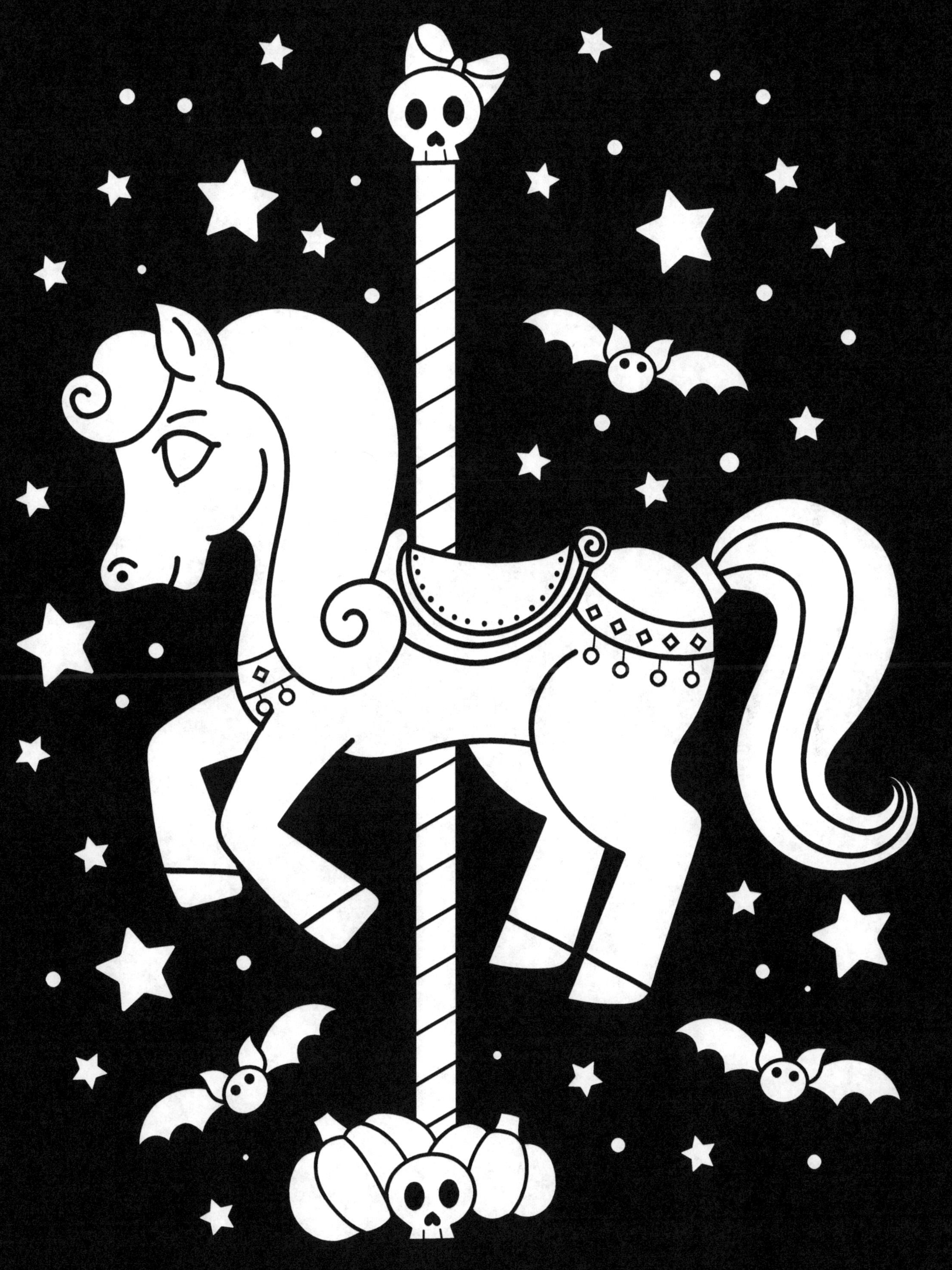

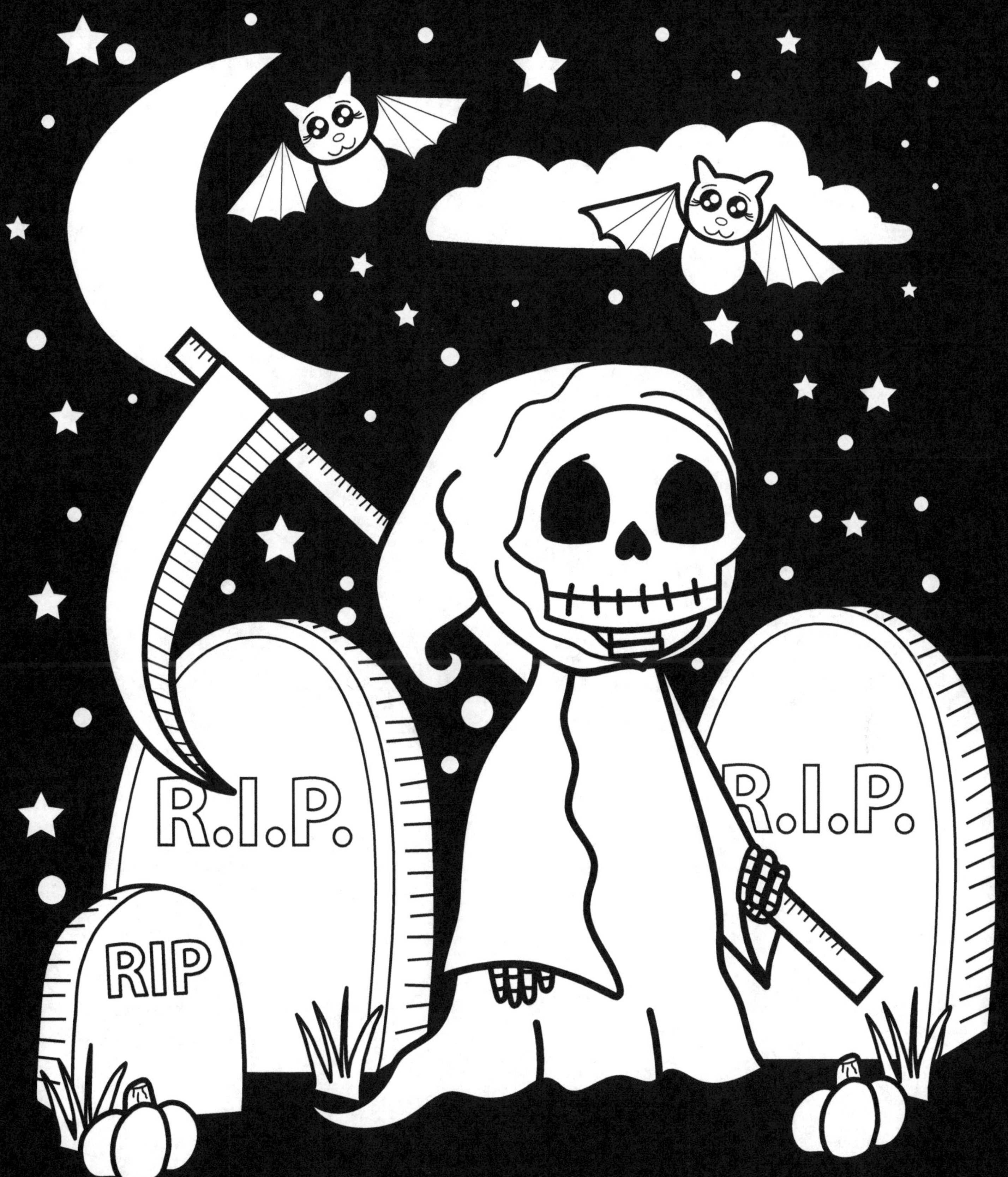
R.I.P.
R.I.P.
RIP

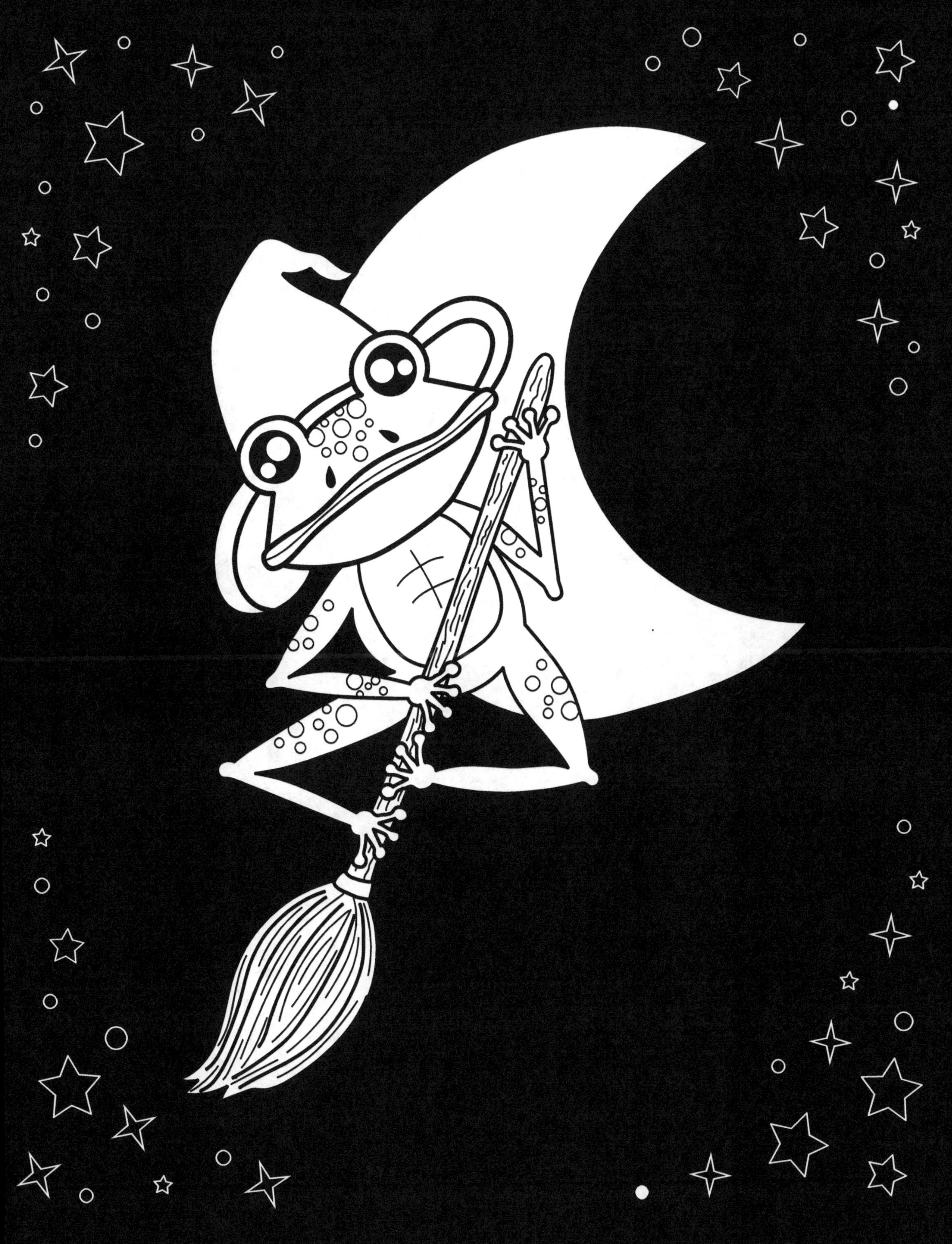

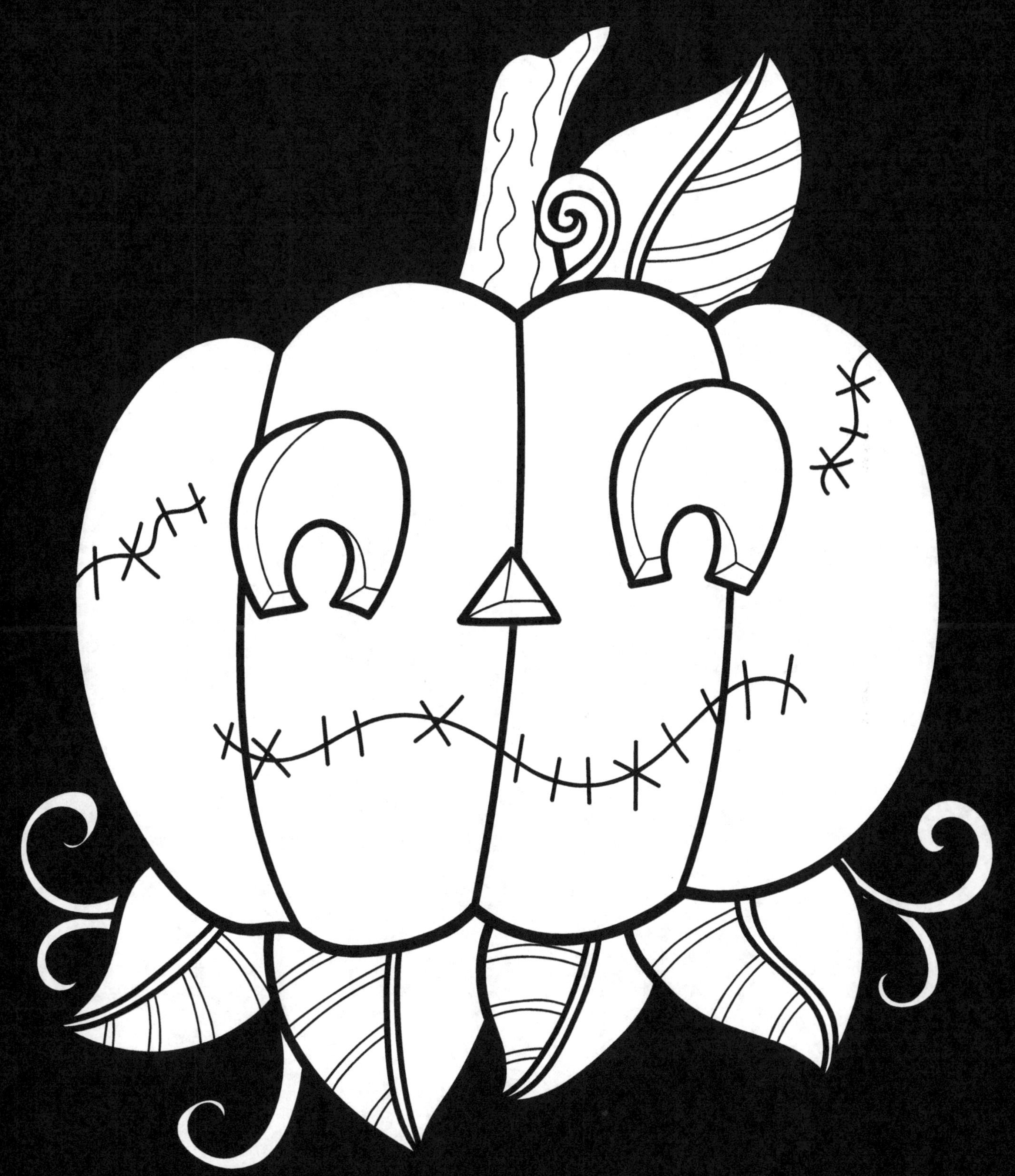

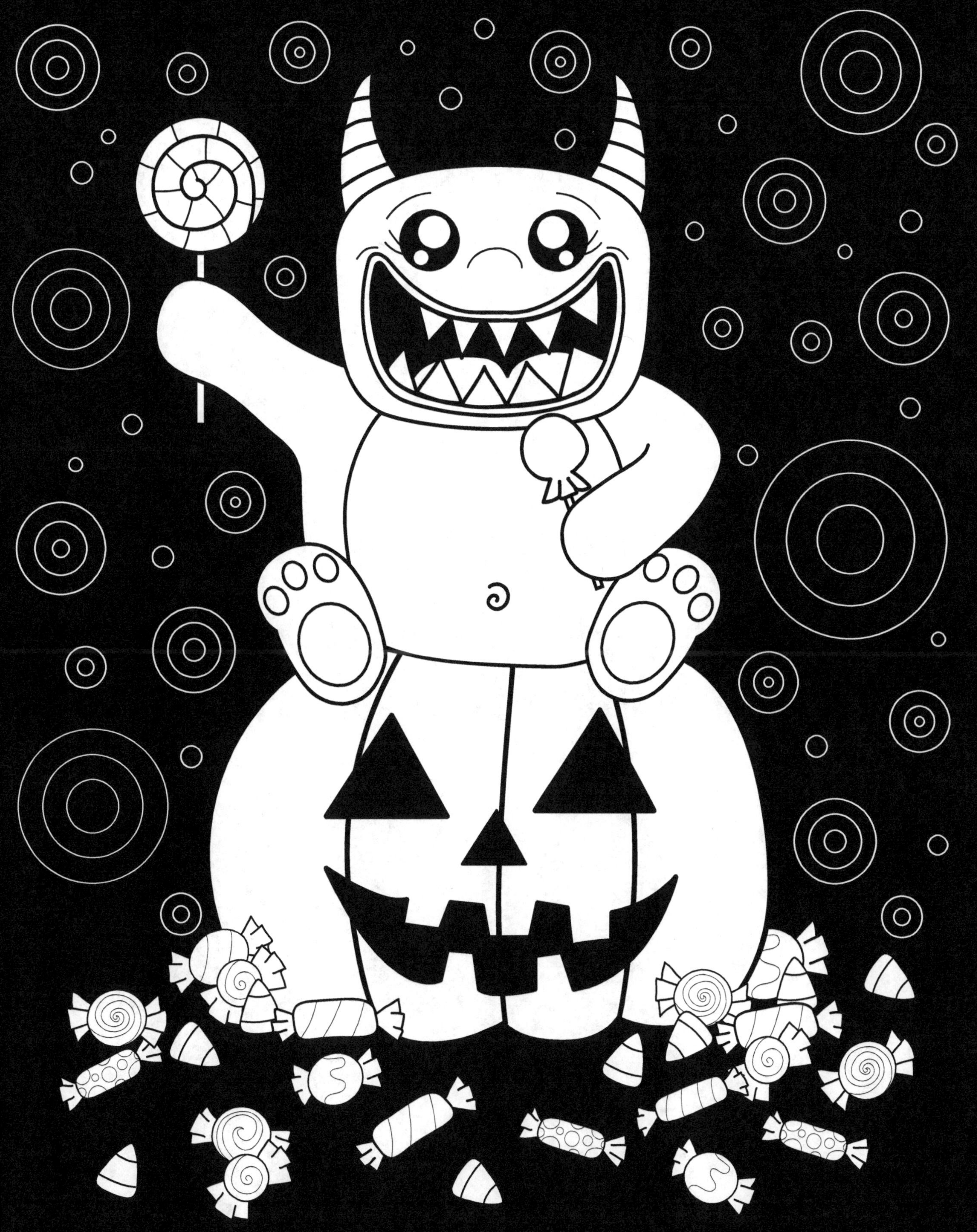

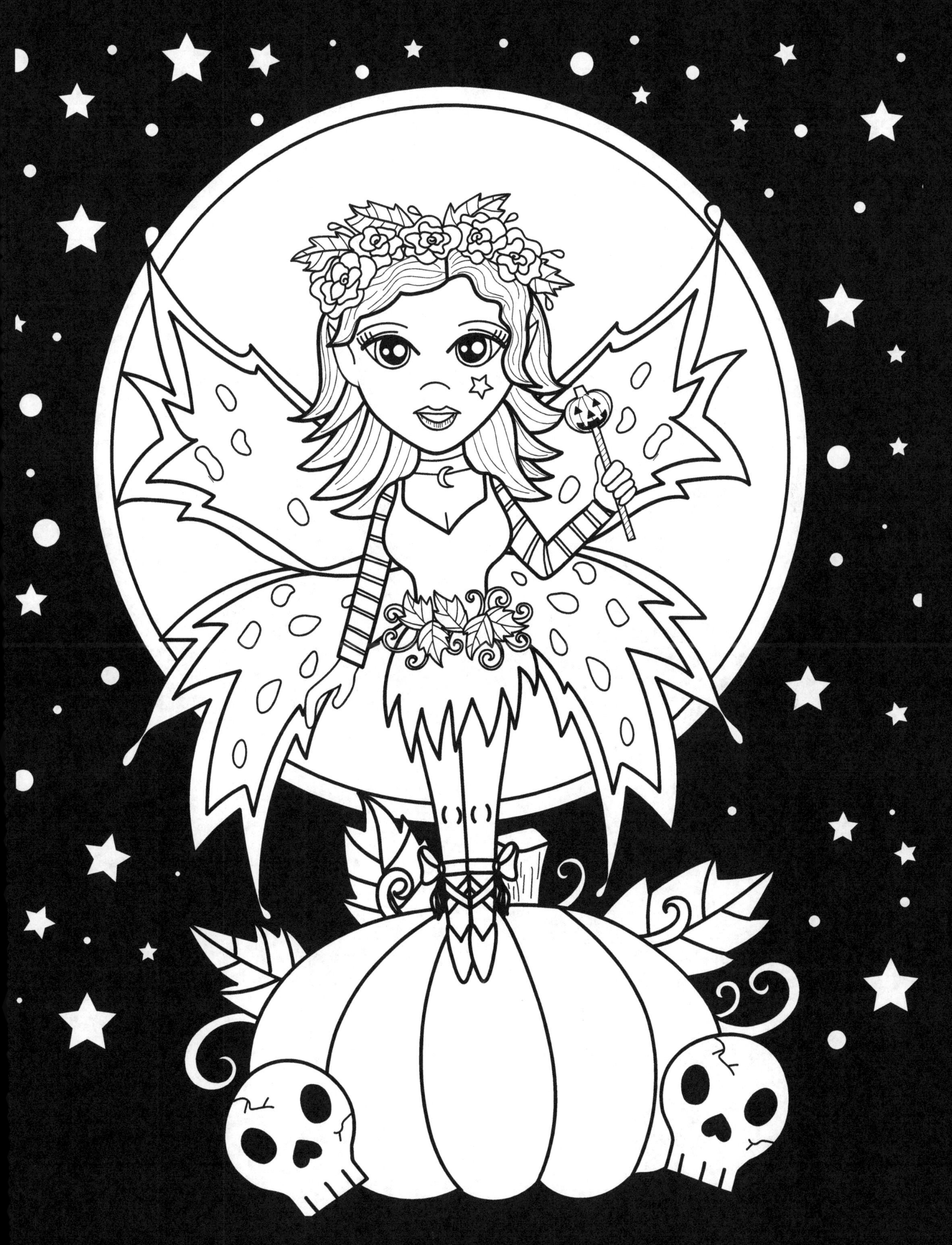

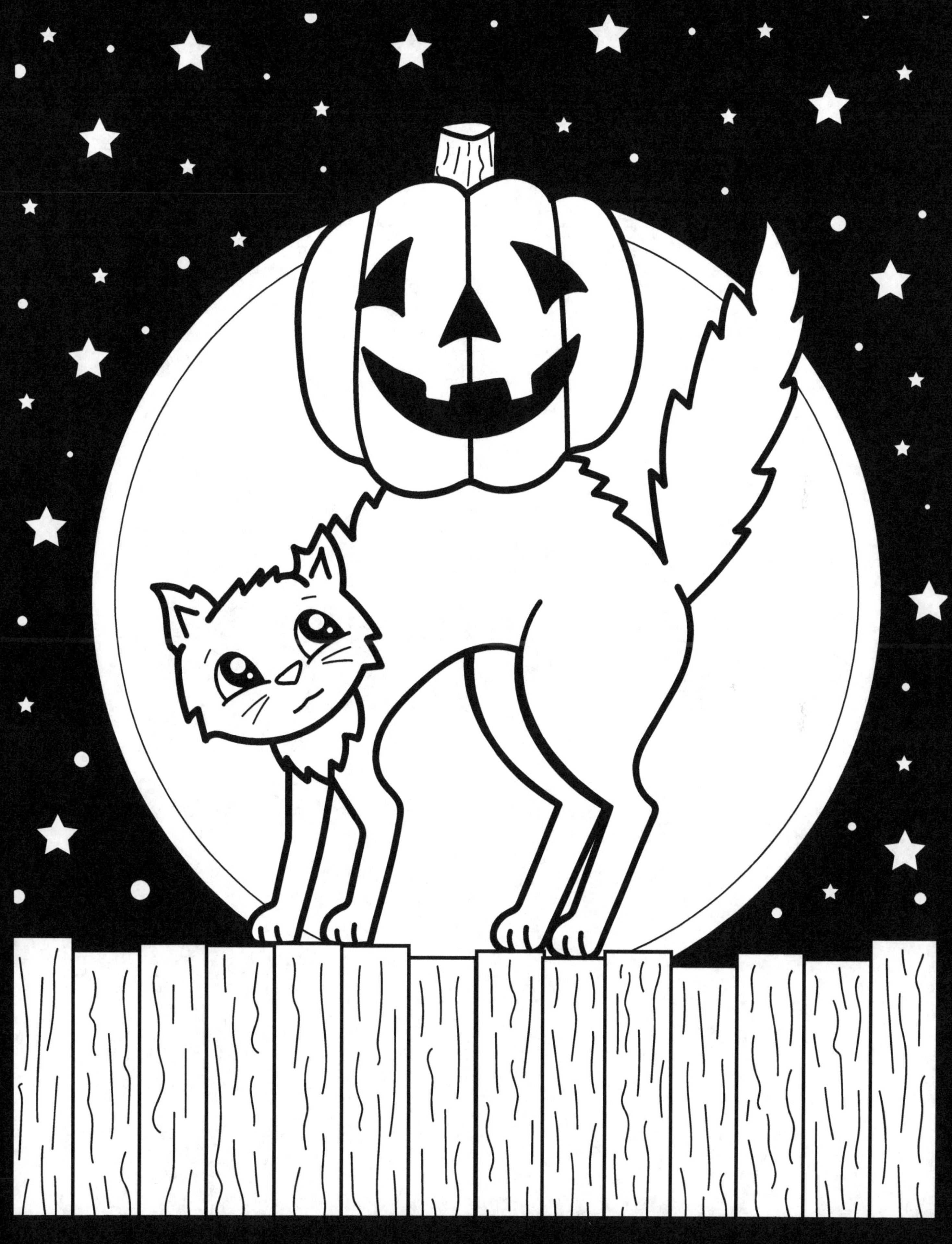

Check out my other books and more on Amazon, Etsy, and www.TheRootsOfDesign.com

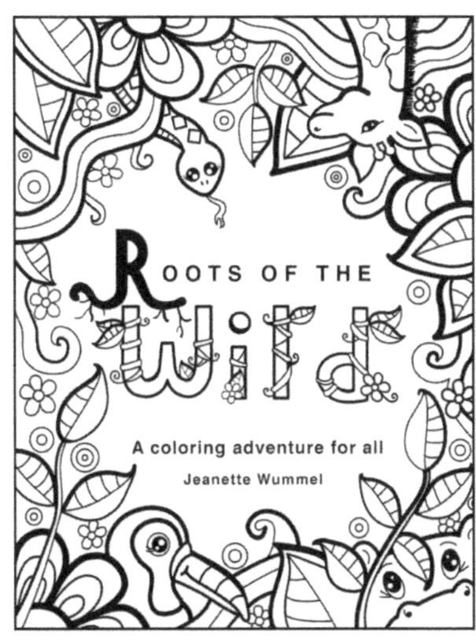

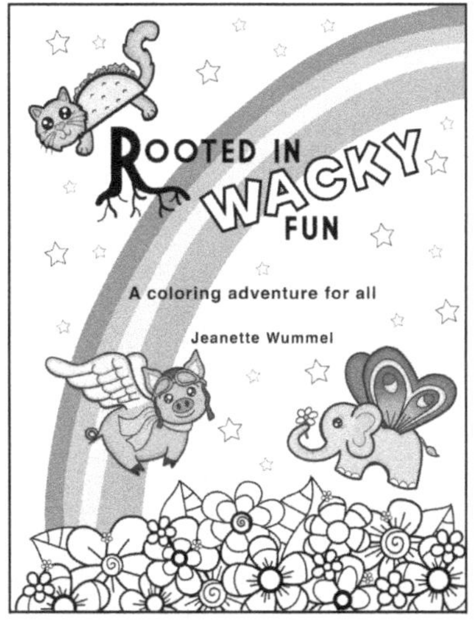

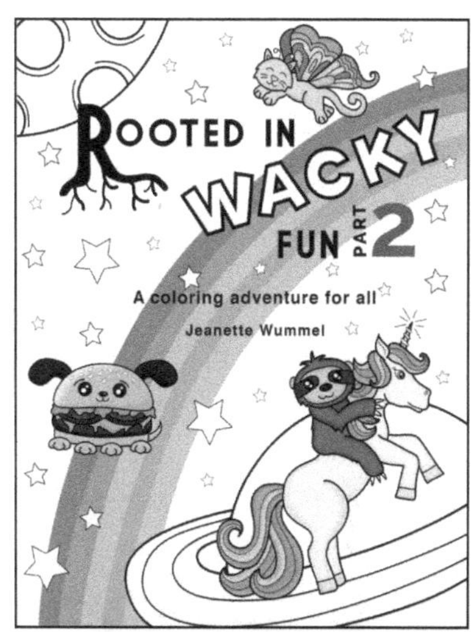

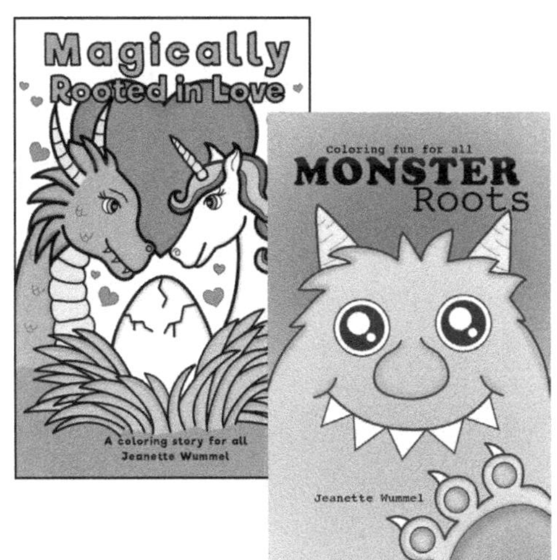

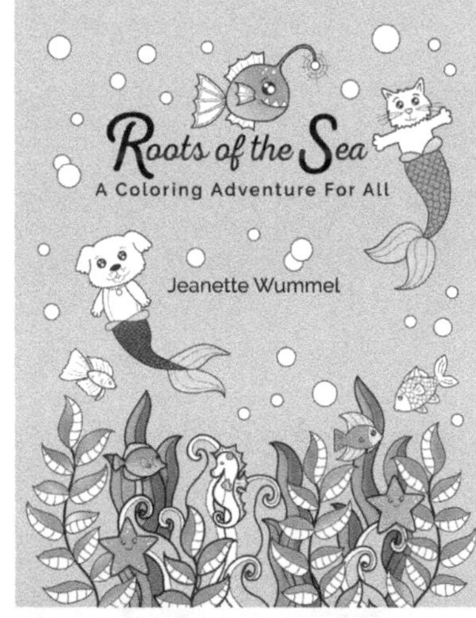

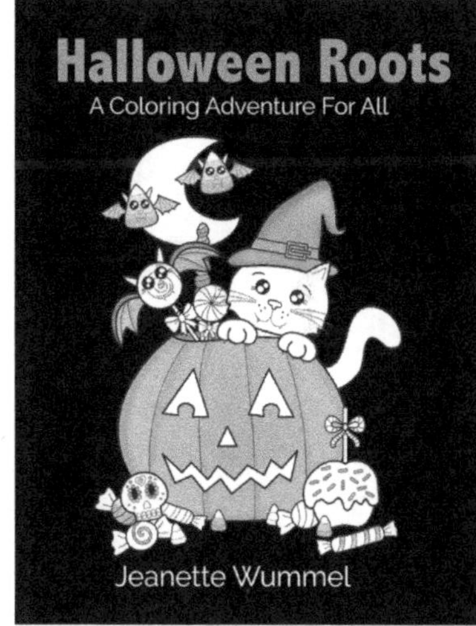

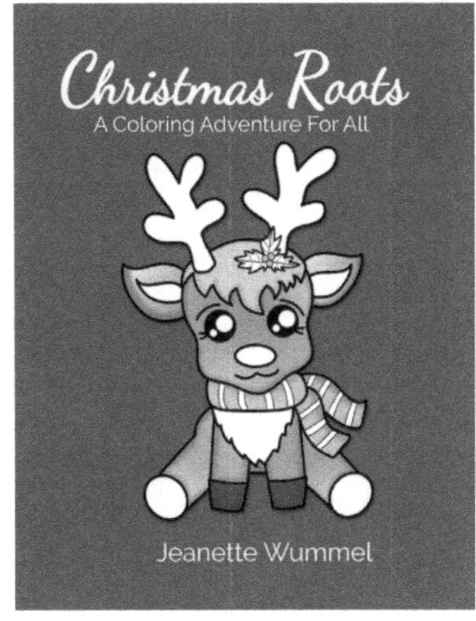

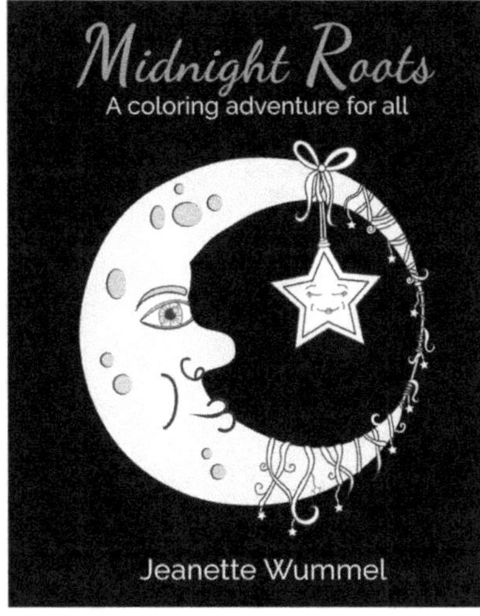

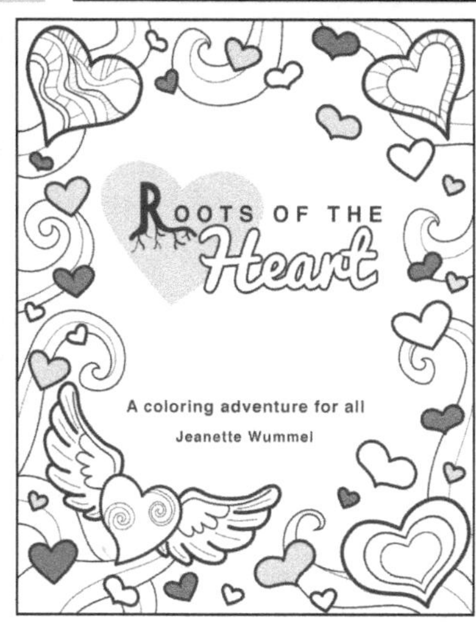

www.ingramcontent.com/pod-product-compliance
Lightning Source LLC
LaVergne TN
LVHW081422110826
845149LV00010B/1839

* 9 7 8 0 9 9 8 2 1 5 2 8 0 *